Currituck Memories and Adventures

Best Wishes

Travis Morris

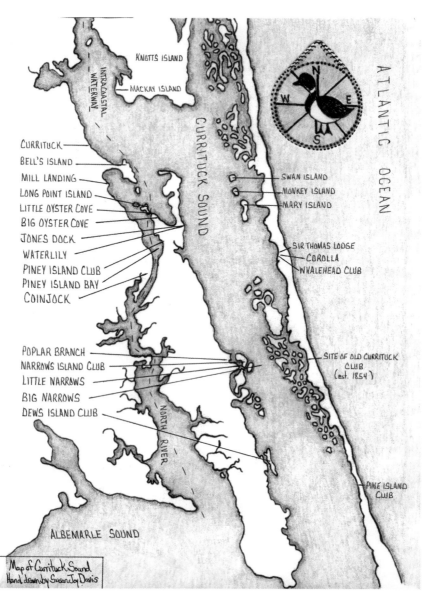

Drawing representing parts of Coinjock Bay, Intracoastal Waterway and Currituck Sound. *Courtesy of Susan Joy Davis.*

Currituck Memories and Adventures

More Tales from a Native Gunner

Travis Morris

Charleston   London

History
PRESS

Published by The History Press
Charleston, SC 29403
www.historypress.net

Copyright © 2007 by Travis Morris
All rights reserved

Cover image: Ronnie Balance, Marvin Doxey and Henry Doxey with gleanings of a good hunt. *Courtesy of Jean Doxey.*

First published 2007

Manufactured in the United Kingdom

ISBN 978.1.59629.305.2

Library of Congress Cataloging-in-Publication Data

Morris, Travis.
  Currituck memories and adventures : more tales from a native gunner / Travis
Morris.
      p. cm.
  ISBN-13: 978-1-59629-305-2 (alk. paper)
  1. Duck shooting--North Carolina--Currituck County--Anecdotes. 2. Fishing--North
Carolina--Currituck County--Anecdotes. 3. Currituck Co. (N.C.)--Social life and
customs. 4. Morris, Travis. I. Title.
  SK333.D8M66 2007
  975.6'132043092--dc22
  [B]
                        2007023334

Notice: The information in this book is true and complete to the best of our knowledge.
It is offered without guarantee on the part of the author or The History Press. The
author and The History Press disclaim all liability in connection with the use of this
book.

This book is dedicated to my old family. *Top photo, front row, left to right*: Rhonda Lee Morris, Wayne Frances Morris, Ruth Travis Morris; *back row, left to right*: Chester Walton Morris, Frances Meiggs Morris and Earl Travis Morris. Frances died of cancer on February 5, 1992. I married Jo Ann Hayman on September 16, 1995. *Author's collection.*

My old family setting out for a relaxing summer afternoon on the *Frances M. Author's collection.*

And to my new family: *Front row, left to right*: April and Amanda Lee, Jo Ann Morris, Travis Morris, Ginger Morris, Chet Morris, Chandler Sawyer, Rhonda Morris, West Ambrose, Ruth Ambrose; *back row, left to right*: Jackie and Lonnie Lee, Walton Morris, Rodney Sawyer, Wayne Sawyer and Cameron Sawyer. *Author's collection.*

Contents

CONTENTS

Why This Book Was Written

After my first book, *Duck Hunting on Currituck Sound: Tales of a Native Gunner*, people kept asking me when I was going to write another one. I decided to do it.

I wrote the stories, but I type with one finger and my spelling is terrible. I wrote my daddy a letter one time when I was at Campbell College and he sent me a book with twenty thousand spelling words!

Susan Joy Davis, who helped me put together my first book, was busy doing something else and didn't have time to help me. I then called on my youngest daughter, Rhonda Lee Morris, who I know is quite capable if she could find the time. She is executive director of Kids First Child Advocacy Center in Elizabeth City. That's a nonprofit that works with abused and neglected children in northeastern North Carolina. She also serves on state

Travis Morris. *Author's collection.*

Rhonda Morris running the *Corolla Express* from Jones Dock in Waterlily to Whalehead Club in Corolla when she was about ten years old. *Author's collection.*

Rhonda editing the book while waiting for Jo Ann's Sunday dinner. *Author's collection.*

Boards of Directors and is a speaker at conferences across the state for various organizations, so she stays busy. Rhonda agreed to help me without a second thought. I think she knew it would be an adventure that she may one day write about!

Introductory Whispers

My daddy, Chester Ralph Morris, grew up as the oldest of nine children on a farm in Gates County, North Carolina. He plowed horses and mules in the summer and worked in the log woods in the winter when he wasn't in school.

He worked his way through Wake Forest College waiting on tables and as a telephone operator. He came to Currituck County, North Carolina, in 1926 and started practicing law. He soon represented many of the old duck hunting clubs in the county. He married my mother, Edna Earl Boswood, in 1927. I was their only child, born November 29, 1932.

When my Granddaddy Boswood died in 1941, we moved from the house Mama and Daddy built in the village of Currituck to Coinjock and lived with my grandmother on her farm. That is where I was raised.

I remember as a little boy sitting out under a big oak tree in the front yard near the road in the summertime about dark, watching the trucks go by heading north with Currituck produce. They were lit up like Christmas trees, and I wondered where they were going. As you will discover in this book, I was to find out before my career was over.

I remember something else as if it were yesterday. I was eight years old. It was in the summertime and I went in Daddy's back office where he was. The same electric fan that is in my son's warehouse was sitting on Daddy's desk blowing.

I told him I needed to talk to him. I told him I knew he wanted me to be a lawyer, but I just couldn't do that. I didn't feel like I was smart enough, plus I just didn't want to do that.

I knew he was disappointed, but he told me I had to do what was right for me. He said any profession that was honest was honorable.

I spent three years in the Coast Guard, January 1951 to January 1954. I married Frances Meiggs on June 21, 1953. When I got out of the Coast Guard, Frances and I both went to Campbell College in Buies Creek, North Carolina, for a year and a half. Frances had been to WCUNC (the Women's College of the University of North Carolina) in Greensboro for a year and had enough credits to graduate. We lived in an eight- by thirty-foot house trailer. To make extra spending money, Frances started a takeout business. She cooked hamburgers, and I delivered them to students on campus.

We came back to Currituck and moved into the house that Mama and Daddy had built in the village of Currituck. We lived there seventeen years, during which time we had a son and three daughters.

Frances's daddy was a farmer and trucker. I wanted to stay in Currituck, and that was the only way I knew I could do that. I rented Granny's farm and some other small farms and raised produce. I bought a truck to haul my own produce, and eventually bought two more trucks. I soon found myself more in the trucking business than I was farming. I also found time to guide sportsmen in the wintertime.

I found out that, to keep truck drivers, I had to give them year-round work, and that meant hauling out of Florida. I farmed and was in the long-distance trucking business from 1956 until 1970, when we started Currituck Realty. Frances and I both got our real estate license in 1968, but I kept the trucks until 1970. Just to be sure I could make it in the real estate business, Frances got a job as district manager for Avon. With four children, we needed a steady income.

In 1973 we converted Frances's daddy's barn into a five-thousand-square-foot house, which made a good place for our children to grow up. Frances was in Currituck Realty with me the last thirteen years of her life. She died of cancer February 5, 1992.

I married Jo Ann Hayman September 16, 1995. Her husband, Jimmy, had died six years previous at the age of forty-four. They had one daughter. Jo Ann took over the hardware and building supply business and is still running it with her daughter, Jackie, and son-in-law, Lonnie.

I'm ten years older than Jo Ann. I dated her sister when we were in high school. After Frances died, Mr. Frank Penn, the man who owned Monkey Island, told me to find me a woman ten years younger than me. He said if I got one any younger I couldn't take care of her and if I got one any older I'd have to wait on her. I took his advice.

If you read my first book, *Duck Hunting on Currituck Sound: Tales from a Native Gunner*, you will know that I ran Monkey Island Club for four years and started Piney Island Club. This was all after I quit farming and trucking. Now you have a few whispers of my past.

In this collection, I will tell a little about commercial fishing in Currituck Sound and tell more duck hunting stories, both as I experienced them and as they were told to me by older men. To give you a picture of what it was like to make a living for many of us in Currituck, I will include a section on my truck farming years that I think you will find interesting. Few people made a living in Currituck doing just one thing. Many of us guided sportsmen and farmed to make ends meet and this will fill out that picture.

There will be some stories about how it was growing up in Currituck in the thirties, forties and fifties. There will be plenty of pictures, just because I like pictures and thought you might enjoy them, too.

Wampuss Cat

While the rest of the stories in this book are true, I thought I would start out with a sure enough "tale" that may or may not be true. Based on some stories I heard my daddy tell when I was a little boy, I tend to think it is true.

When I got to Piney Island Hunt Club the other night, Jimmy Markert said he had a story to tell DeWitt McCotter and me, but he made us wait until he could go take a shower and everybody had gathered around.

Things happened like this: On the evening of January 7, 1988, the day the snowstorm came through, John Williams and Dal Barber were hunting together. It is told that they had consumed quite a bit of Old Mr. Boston peach brandy, especially Dal. When they got in, they discovered they needed something from the store. They went over to the Coinjock Marina. Now,

We never got the "Wampuss Cat," but I think this must be what he looked like. John Williams killed this particular cat in Texas in 2006. *Courtesy of John Williams.*

June Twiford cooking the dinner that John Williams was craving. *Author's collection.*

mind you, the old lady is really "picking geese" (snowing hard). On the way back, they turned into Piney Island Road and, as they rounded the first curve, the headlights shone on a herd of deer in the first mowed field on the left. They saw one deer that, at first, seemed to have his head caught in the fence. John pulled the Blazer into the field to shine the lights on the deer and, lo and behold, what they saw was a deer with a big wildcat on him. Dal jumped out of the Blazer with his pen knife in the ready position. He pulled his sleeves down and his hood over his head. He stabbed that pen knife into the wildcat, whereupon the cat jumped straight up and Dal stabbed him two more times on the way up!

All this time, John Williams was sitting in the Blazer, just watching. He said all he could think about was the good fried chicken June was cooking that he was sure going to miss because he knew he would have to take Dal to the emergency room when that cat got through with him.

Jimmy and Fred Dunstan said John and Dal came running into the house telling this story and that the knife was bloody. June Twiford and Tammy Stone (cooks at the club) also confirmed this in the story they told. June said they were so excited they could hardly eat. As soon as they finished, Jimmy, Fred, John and Dal all went back to the scene to look for tracks. Of course, it was snowing so hard they couldn't even find the tracks of the Blazer. But, listen carefully, here is the one thing that makes me think there might be something to the story: Jim and Fred both said that, in the ditch where the brush was keeping the snow from covering up the tracks, you could see the tracks of a big cat that was running. Also, Jewel and Sam, the hunting dogs, picked up on a hot trail. The boys followed them a good way into the woods, but finally called them out.

John Williams said he had coon hunted a lot and had seen a lot of bobcats, but never anything like this. He said when the cat was on that deer he stretched from the back of the deer's head to his rump. I used to hear my daddy and some of the older men tell stories about a Wampuss Cat that was around here. Frankly, I think those boys got tangled up with him.

Folks, you can make your own decision about this story. I am just relating it to you the way it was told to me. There is one thing for sure. If Dal Barber attacked that big cat with a pen knife, he had a lot of Old Mr. Boston in him or else he has a lot more nerve than I think he has!

Duck Hunting with Barbara Brumsey Smith

There were several of us around the village of Currituck who were real close friends, and the ones of us living are still close, though we are scattered from here to Atlanta. There were eight of us boys that made Eagle Scout at the same time in 1948. When we had our fiftieth reunion in 1998, we invited Barbara.

Barbara was the only child of Mr. Carl and Miss Tommie Brumsey. Her daddy was a successful farmer at the time we were growing up. Her mother was teaching school.

It's important to tell you a little about Barbara Glen Brumsey Smith's mother, Miss Tommie Brumsey, who taught the first grade in Currituck County schools for forty-two years. She taught many who will read this, including me. You will see how this ties in with duck hunting.

Left to right: Dodson Mathias, Barbara Smith and Travis Morris, fifty-seven years after we were marooned at Long Point. This photo was taken by Jo Ann Morris at her cottage in Corolla. *Courtesy of Jo Ann Morris.*

Knapp house at Mackey Island. *Courtesy of Wildlife Resource Center*.

Boathouse and the boat *Bootlegger* at Mackey Island. *Courtesy of Wildlife Resource Center*.

Mr. Joseph Palmer Knapp. *Courtesy of Kevin Doxey.*

Mrs. Margaret Rutledge Knapp. *Courtesy of Kevin Doxey.*

Miss Tommie came to Currituck as a result of Mr. Joseph Palmer Knapp. He was a very wealthy man from Brooklyn, New York, who came to Currituck duck hunting. In 1918, he bought Mackey Island and made Currituck County his permanent residence. He said North Carolina needed his tax money more than New York did.

In 1932, Mr. Knapp gave Currituck County more money than the people of Currituck County paid in county taxes, mostly to the schools. He built Knapp School and houses for teachers to live in next to each of the schools at Currituck, Poplar Branch, Moyock and Knotts Island. These were locally called "teacherages." He was also responsible for Currituck having its first school lunch program, music and arts programs and many other benefits not found in other schools in the state. Mr. Knapp also founded the Currituck Farmer's Exchange (a cooperative operation) during the Depression. It was duck hunting that had brought him to Currituck in the first place and he contributed to the preservation of good duck hunting through the founding of More Game Birds in America, which later became Ducks Unlimited.

Mr. Knapp had a close friend in Russell Griggs, who I will speak of later as the owner of Hampton Lodge and the Croatan Hotel. Mr. Knapp got the school board to hire Miss Maude C. Newbury as superintendent and told her to recruit good teachers. He said he would pay them $100 a month supplement in addition to the $100 a month the state paid them. That was good money in those days.

Miss Newbury hired Tommie Gregory, who was twenty years old in 1922. Miss Newbury recruited her from Middle Tennessee College. That's how Barbara's mother came to be in Currituck; her daddy, Mr. Carl, was a native.

Barbara's daddy had money when we were growing up; cabbage, snap beans and Irish potatoes were selling. He bought her a new 1948 Roadmaster Buick. She was the only one in our crowd who had her own car. She would pick up a load of us and we'd just ride around or we'd go to Elizabeth City to the movies. Elizabeth City had the nearest movie. It was twenty miles, but we had a great time.

One day Barbara (who is still a good shot), Dodson Mathias and I were going hunting on the east side of Coinjock Bay. The wind was blowing hard from the northwest.

We left Mill Landing at Maple that morning before light in my fourteen-foot skiff with a seven-horsepower Champion outboard motor. When day broke, a strong northwester came with it, but we were already tied out and in the blind. I don't remember how many ducks we killed, but one time going out to retrieve a duck, we got a decoy string caught in the propeller

Mr. Russell Griggs. *Courtesy of Kevin Doxey.*

Mr. Carl and Miss Tommie Brumsey. *Courtesy of Barbara Brumsey Smith.*

and broke the shear pin. We didn't have any more shear pins or tools with us. Lesson learned. We drifted and poled over to Long Point Island, which was just about 250 yards. Now remember this was a very cold day. It was just above freezing, but we had plenty of food. Granny saw to that.

We walked over to the east side of Long Point. The Intracoastal Waterway (ICW) runs right beside the island there. We were hoping a boat would come along, but no such luck. We started shooting, thinking somebody would hear us. No luck.

In the meantime, Barbara's daddy got to worrying about us because the wind was blowing so hard. He went and got Lionel Boswood, who was the local game warden at the time, to go check on us. The game warden boat was an open flat-bottom tunnel boat with a flat-head V8 Ford motor. Lionel kept the boat at Mill Landing. Since the wind was blowing from the west, we could hear the boat coming. We made it back to the west side of the island by the time Lionel got there. We were glad to see him!

Another time, after Barbara and I were both married but before she moved away, we went out on a cold blowy day with the wind strong from the northeast. The sky was overcast and freezing every drop that was flying. Barbara wanted to go duck hunting. She thought they'd be flying. I told her the tide was too low and we couldn't get the boat out. She kept right on, "Yes we can." As usual, I gave in and said, "All right, we'll try it." At the time I had a little dead-rise boat I kept on a trailer with a forty-horsepower Scott-Atwater outboard motor.

We put over at a ramp right behind the Maple Inn. When we got to the end of the ditch there was no water…just like I had told her. Barbara said, "Oh come on, we can pull it across the flat." We both had hip boots on, so we got out of the boat and started trying to pull the boat across the flat. The bottom was a little muddy, and I got both feet stuck in the mud and fell flat on my face in the mud and water. Needless to say, that ended the hunting trip.

Now, back at home, something else was happening. I was in the farming and long-distance trucking business at that time. I had just gotten my common carrier license. With that kind of license, the state auditor checked your books once a year. While Barbara and I were out, the state auditor came looking for me. Frances told him I was out duck hunting with my girlfriend. Frances said the auditor looked at her kind of funny when she told him that. Then she tried to explain that Barbara and I had always been good friends and we often hunted together. About that time, Barbara and I rolled up with me looking like a tar baby. It was quite embarrassing.

The hunting trip I just told you about was just before Barbara moved away from Currituck. After college, Barbara had married Millard Smith.

Barbara Smith and my son-in-law, West Ambrose, after a good day's hunt. *Author's collection.*

He worked for U.S. Gypsum. They moved to Fanwood, New Jersey, where he commuted to his office on Madison Avenue in New York City.

When they lived there, I was in the trucking business. On my way back from New York one time, Barbara wanted to come home with me. She said she had to bring the dog. I said okay, figuring I'd put him in the trailer. I told her to meet me at a service area on the New Jersey Turnpike at a certain time. When I got there she was there with that little old dog I had planned to put in the trailer. Nothing doing. That dog had to ride to Currituck in the cab with us.

Barbara and Millard later moved from New Jersey to Boston, where Millard was a plant manager. Then they moved to Marion, Virginia, and then to Chicago. After Millard retired, they moved back to Currituck and we started duck hunting again.

Barbara is as anxious to get out on the water and hunt today as she was when we were youngsters. She hunts regularly now with my son-in-law, West Ambrose, so if you see a white-headed woman out in the Currituck Sound on a blustery day, you can be pretty sure it's Barbara Brumsey Smith.

A Brand-new Toy for an Old Gunner

The first gun I had of my very own, a Model 11 Remington, was owned by Mr. Joseph Palmer Knapp. He gave the gun to Mr. Frank Brumsey in the early twenties. In the late twenties, Daddy bought the gun from Mr. Frank for sixty-five dollars.

One day in the early forties, Daddy was hunting at the Whalehead Club with Mr. Ray T. Adams, owner of the club. Daddy was his attorney. They were shooting ducks and Daddy's gun was hanging up (it wouldn't eject the shell). Mr. Adams told Daddy to throw the gun overboard. Daddy told him he couldn't do that; it was the only gun he had. In about two weeks, Daddy received a brand-new Belgium Browning automatic in the mail from Mr. Adams.

At that point, Daddy gave me the old Model 11 Remington. That is the only gun I ever had of my own until 2003. The guns I had before that were borrowed 410 single-barrel hammer guns. One gun that I had, Martin Simpson Jr., who was a good friend of my daddy's, let me use. When his son Bland, who is the author of several books, got old enough to use it, I gave it back to him. The other 410 was lent to me by Steve Nimmocks, whose daddy was Judge Q.K. Nimmocks from Fayetteville. When Steve's son got old enough to use it, I gave the gun back to Steve. I don't remember which gun I got first. Martin Jr.'s was the prettiest, but it was hard to cock. I had to take both thumbs to cock it. Steve's didn't look too good, but I could cock it with one thumb.

When I got Mr. Knapp's Remington from Daddy, I was proud to have a gun of my very own. I'm not a good shot by any stretch of the imagination, but I have killed many ducks with that gun. One day three years ago, my grandson, Chet Morris, and I were hunting up on the north end of Piney Island. A bunch of ducks came to us. Chet killed his and my gun hung up. Chet said, "Granddaddy, it's time to put that gun in a glass case and buy you a new gun." I thought about it and decided he was right. I went to Currituck Sports and got Ed and Sybil O'Neal to order me a new Model 1187 Remington automatic shotgun.

In the spring, my other grandson, Chandler Sawyer, who works for the North Carolina Wildlife Resources Commission's Educational Center (WRCEC) in Corolla, told me they had room for a gun there and asked if I wanted to lend my old gun to the center. I said I would. Chandler and Sharon Mead, who is the curator there, researched the serial number of my gun and found out it was made in 1906. If I had known that gun was ninety-seven years old, I'd have been scared to death to shoot it. I'd had electrical tape around the screw that holds the stock on for as long as I can remember. It's so worn out the screw won't stay in without the tape.

That old gun is on display now in the Wildlife Education Center in Corolla, where it can't do any harm.

Sometimes it's a good idea to take the advice of your grandchildren!

Hampton Lodge

Hampton Lodge is located at the very north end of Churches Island (Waterlily), where the campground is today. This land was owned by Pierce Hampton from the 1800s until he died in the early 1900s. That's where the name Hampton Lodge came from. Mr. Hampton was in the North Carolina House of Representatives from 1887–89, 1907–11 and again in 1915.

It was said that Mr. Hampton was one of the best duck hunters in eastern North Carolina. Pierce loved to talk about the days when he "and Grover Cleveland could kill more ducks than any hunters in the country." Cleveland sailed from Washington, D.C., to Currituck Sound to hunt ducks and Pierce Hampton was his guide, philosopher and friend.

Mr. Pierce Hampton. *Courtesy of Kevin Doxey*.

The last of the market hunters, Van and Russell Griggs. Mrs. Knapp had this picture painted and gave it to Miss Bernie and Mr. Russell for Christmas in 1954. *Courtesy of Kevin Doxey.*

Pierce Hampton's daughter, Bernie, married Russell Griggs. He and his brother Van were said to be two of the best market hunters on Currituck Sound. Van held the record for killing the most ducks in one day on the sound: 892.

After Mr. Knapp bought Mackey Island, he hired Mr. Russell Griggs as his guide. Not only was Mr. Russell his guide, but he was also one of Mr. Knapp's best friends. Plus, he knew Mr. Russell was one of the best shots in Currituck and he liked to match skills with him.

Miss Bernie inherited her daddy's property, and they started Hampton Lodge after market hunting was outlawed. Miss Bernie was always interested and active in politics. They had a lot of politicians come to Currituck to hunt from Hampton Lodge. I remember my Granddaddy Boswood telling me about one time he was going duck hunting with Mr. Russell Griggs. They were both good shots. This was in the days when you loaded your own brass shells. The night before they were to go hunting, my Aunt Sarah loaded the shells for my granddaddy. The next morning, Granddaddy and Mr. Russell went out in the sound and tied out. They got in the blind and the ducks started coming. Mr. Russell was killing ducks and my granddaddy couldn't touch a feather. He was really flustered. He finally took the end out of a shell to see what kind of shot Sarah had put in there. He found she had loaded his shells with buck shot. The words he had for her I'm sure could not be printed here!

The Griggses built the Croatan Hotel in Kill Devil Hills around 1930. This was one of the first hotels in the Kitty Hawk–Kill Devil Hills–Nags Head area. Now Miss Bernie and Mr. Russell had a place for their guests to stay in the summertime. Two of their regular guests were Lindsey Warren (congressman from North Carolina and later comptroller general of the United States) and Congressman Herbert Bonner.

Mr. Russell took his old thirty-two-foot gas boat down to the creek that runs beside the causeway to Manteo so he could take his guests fishing at Oregon Inlet. There was no Oregon Inlet Fishing Center or road to Oregon Inlet then.

Mr. Russell and Miss Bernie eventually sold Hampton Lodge to Tom and Susie Briggs and a group of others and moved to the beach. They built a house right next door to the Croatan on the north side.

In the summer of 1955, when the Briggses owned the Croatan, Frances and I worked there. She was day clerk and I was night clerk. The room they gave us to stay in was kind of like an attic. It was right over the lobby. There was no air conditioning. It was so hot up there some days I couldn't sleep. Since I had the night shift, I had to sleep days. I would take a little skiff out in Kitty Hawk Bay and tie it to a tree right at the edge of the water and sleep in the bottom of the skiff under the shade of that tree.

Above: Hampton Lodge. *Courtesy of Kevin Doxey.*

Left: Bar and bartender at Hampton Lodge. *Courtesy of Kevin Doxey.*

Above: Croatan Hotel, as viewed from the beach in 1938. *Courtesy of Kevin Doxey.*

Right: Jimmie Gray at the Croatan Hotel, circa 1941. Mr. Russell and Miss Bernie Griggs had no children; they raised Jimmie as their own. *Courtesy of Kevin Doxey.*

The dining room of the Croatan. I can still smell the salt air and sense the comfortable atmosphere of the place. *Courtesy of Kevin Doxey.*

Patrons enjoying drinks and a game of Scrabble at the Croatan in the early forties. *Courtesy of Kevin Doxey.*

Mr. Russell Griggs with mule and cart and Chesapeake Bay retriever. The cart was made from the rear end of an old car. Many people called them "Hoover carts" during the Depression because, when they couldn't afford to fix their cars, they made these carts out of them. In this case, I'm sure Mr. Russell wanted the wide tires of the cart for use in the sand. *Courtesy of Kevin Doxey.*

Jimmie Gray and friends gathered around her *Beachcomber*, circa 1941. *Courtesy of Kevin Doxey.*

Mr. Lindsey Warren, *left*, and Mr. Herbert Bonner. *Courtesy of Kevin Doxey.*

Above: Mr. Russell Griggs's gas boat, the *Croatan*, built in 1927. This picture was taken in 1974, when I owned the boat. Friends, *left to right*, Hambone Twiford, Herbert Lange, Shirley Austin and I had been to Corolla fishing and had caught these big blue fish in the surf. *Author's collection.*

Right: Miss Bernie Griggs. *Courtesy of Kevin Doxey.*

Left to right: Mr. Russell Griggs, Mrs. Margaret Knapp, Miss Bernie Griggs and Jimmie Gray. *Courtesy of Kevin Doxey.*

Frances and I both had off between 5:00 and 7:00 p.m. Miss Bernie would invite us over to their house a lot of evenings to have "Starboard Lights," as she called them: Crème de Menthe.

I remember Mrs. Knapp spent a month at the Croatan Hotel the summer we worked there. She and Miss Bernie were as close of friends as Mr. Knapp and Mr. Russell had been.

Gathering Tales

I remember one time Daddy and I went hunting with Mr. Charlie Wright (Dr. Charles Wright's daddy). We probably left from Deep Creek (behind the Cotton Gin in Jarvisburg) and hunted in Dew's Quarter Bay. I can't remember if we were hunting from a float rig or bush blind that day. This was in the forties. Mr. Dan'l Wright was along too. The gas boat we were in was about thirty feet long with a right good-sized cabin on her that had a kerosene heater in it. I remember it was a clear, cold, windy day. That means the wind was probably out of the northwest. We laid up under the marsh most of the day with the gas boat out of the wind. I didn't get too far from that heater and enjoyed listening to the men spin yarns. As I got older, I started paying closer attention to those stories and realized how important they were to Currituck's history. I started writing my own accounts of trips and recording hunting and fishing stories from some of the older hunters. The next few stories are based on a recorded interview with Henry Doxey. I've known Henry all my life. We both had a good time talking. I wish I had space to include more of the things he told me. Let me introduce you to Henry before relaying his tales.

Henry was born in Currituck in 1923. He is a colorful character who has done a little of everything: he's been a commercial fisherman, a merchant marine, he's run a hunting rig, driven a truck, worked at the Ford plant, been captain of a tugboat when the Chesapeake Bay Bridge tunnel was being built and many other things.

Henry married Jean Doxey, whose father, Captain Lloyd Doxey, was captain of the stern-wheeler *Currituck*, which used to run from Norfolk to Poplar Branch with a stop at Munden's Point. It picked up freight and passengers and carried them to Norfolk, where fish and produce was loaded on trains to go to Northern markets. Captain Lloyd was also captain of the first police boat they had in Hampton Roads. They used that boat to catch bootleggers during Prohibition. Lloyd was captain of the *Annie L. Vansciver*, which carried freight and passengers to and from Elizabeth City with stops at Newbern's Landing in Currituck on the North River side, Nags Head

Henry Doxey. *Courtesy of Kevin Doxey.*

The *Currituck* tied up in Norfolk, Virginia. She replaced the *Comet*. In fact, they took the steam engine out of the *Comet* and used it in the *Currituck*. Tied alongside the *Currituck* in this picture is the *Commodore*, a little freight boat that went in to places like Maple and Barco landings. *Courtesy of Jean Doxey*.

Captain Lloyd Doxey (in the pilot house) was captain of the first police boat they had in Hampton Roads (1920). He stayed on her until 1925. Their job was chasing bootleggers. *Courtesy of Jean Doxey*.

The *Annie L. VanSciver. Courtesy of Jean Doxey.*

and Manteo. He was also captain of the *Trenton*. Henry and Jean had three children: Sharon, Marvin and Kevin. Marvin is the only one who is a hunter and fisherman.

Stranded in Coinjock Bay

Henry Doxey asked if I ever heard about the night he and several others (Melvin Doxey, Numa Barnard, Caleb Walker, Charlie Snowden and Norval Walker) got stranded in Coinjock Bay and nearly froze to death. I said, "Yes, but I've forgotten the details. Refresh my memory." He said Norval Walker was running the boat and he ran her aground. He was about two-thirds lit, like he always stayed. It was at Long Point, where the old Coast Guard base used to be. They couldn't get the boat off ground for a while. When they finally did, she wouldn't start. Norval was the only one in the bunch who had hip boots on. He was going to take them all ashore on his back. Melvin was on Norval's back when he fell down head first in the water. They all finally got to Long Point and built a fire. They were about to freeze to death. The Intracoastal Waterway runs right beside Long Point. After a while a tug came by, and they waved her down. The captain stopped and picked them up. The men on the tug got them in the engine room, got them warmed up and dried off and put them off in Great Bridge.

Now you have to remember that, while all this was going on, the word spread through the community like wildfire that these fellows hadn't come in from hunting. Mr. Will Doxey (Henry and Melvin's daddy) had a boat then and, by the crack of dawn the next morning he was in the bay looking for them.

Mr. Will went to the blind where he knew the missing hunters often went. He found his old number 10 shotgun that Melvin was using and an old single barrel that one of the other boys had. Then Mr. Will found the boat at Long Point. He looked all over Long Point and everywhere he could think of and couldn't find them. Everyone figured they were drowned. I could sure relate to how Mr. Will must have felt from searching for my own children and others when I thought they were lost in the sound.

Mr. Will Doxey. *Courtesy of Henry Doxey.*

About 9:30 the morning after their disappearance, the phone rang in Mr. Emest Taylor's store in Maple and it was Melvin. He said they were in Great Bridge and wanted Mr. Will to come and get them. I know the relief that must have been to the community.

Outboard Motor Blues

Henry Doxey said nobody had an outboard motor around here in the thirties. A fellow named Russell Box owned an appliance store in Elizabeth City and he was kind of backing Charlie Snowden in the hunting lodge. Russell and Charlie bought a Sea King outboard motor from Culpepper Hardware. They put that motor on a skiff. Then *everybody* wanted a motor.

About the third time they used it, Charlie was short of guides and had to go across the sound himself to guide. The wind was blowing hard from the northeast. He asked Henry if he would guide Russell Box that day, saying he'd have an outboard motor. Henry said he was tickled to get to run that outboard motor.

Henry tied out between Little Bells Island and Made Island in Coinjock Bay. Soon some swan came flapping along. It was not legal to shoot swan at that time.

"We better not shoot them," Henry said.

"Yeah, I'm gonna get me one of 'em. We got a motor. You can hide him in the marsh." So Russell cut two out of the bunch. Henry went out to pick them up and hit something and broke one blade off the propeller.

They decided they better take up and go on in. Just before they got to Mill Landing in Maple, the motor said, "WAAAAAAAAAAAA."

"We must have lost the other blade off the propeller," Henry said. He cut the motor off and tipped it up and the whole lower unit was gone. It had vibrated the bolts loose and fell off. Henry and Russell poled on in. That was the end of outboard number one.

A Doxey Father/Son Hunting Trip and More Motor Blues

Henry Doxey and his son Marvin were out there in Coinjock Bay in a blind. It was slick calm. Blackbirds were flying all around them.

"Daddy, why don't you shoot some of those blackbirds?" Marvin asked.

"I can't shoot them with #2 shot," his daddy responded.

Marvin said, "Here, I'll fix you a shell." He cut open the end of a shell, dumped the shot out and looked in his daddy's lunchbox, where he found some tacks, grains of corn and stock peas. He filled the shell up with that, crimped it and said, "Here, put that in her." Henry put it in his gun and forgot about it. By then, of course, the blackbirds had quit flying.

A little later, nine geese came flapping along just above the water.

"Marvin, get down and don't move," Henry told his son. Two of the geese broke off and lit just outside the decoys. The other seven lit just a little farther out. The first two were just about close enough to shoot. Henry told Marvin, "Get ready and put it right on his head." Then he glanced up and saw the other seven paddling just as hard as they could for the decoys. He said, "Wait a minute. The others are coming." They were soon close enough.

Henry said, "All right. Put it right on his head now." Marvin did. He pulled the trigger and BAM, the old goose fell right over dead. The other geese jumped up and Henry put it on one and pulled the trigger: POOF. "God Almighty knows," Henry told me, "I tried to get another shell in that gun, but the geese were gone."

Marvin said, "Daddy, why didn't you kill that goose?"

"That shell you gave me was no ---- good. If you ever do that to me again, you ain't going hunting with me no more."

A little later that same day, Henry and Marvin were out of the blind riding around and they saw Charlie Snowden and Russell Box coming to them.

"How about using your gun?" Charlie asked. "I was taking the plug out of mine and the spring flew overboard."

Left to right: Ronnie Balance, Marvin Doxey and Henry Doxey with gleanings of a good hunt. *Courtesy of Jean Doxey*.

"You can use it," Henry said, "but be careful. Don't point it at anybody. Sometimes it'll shoot one time and sometimes both barrels will go off at the same time."

"Well, that's better than nothing."

It wasn't long before Henry saw Charlie and Russell poling toward them. Henry went to meet them to see what was wrong. That gun had gone off and gone through the carburetor and come out the back of the motor. You could see the piston. Henry said the words they were saying couldn't be printed here. End of motor number two.

Russell Box said, "Boy, I'm going to buy you a decent gun." When Marvin got a little older, Charlie bought Marvin a Browning Sweet 16 with a gold trigger.

Catfish Frenzy

In the late thirties and early forties, Henry Doxey was running a long-net fishing rig out of Currituck for Charlie Snowden. Charlie had three rigs, Mr. Lou Brumsey had one, Mr. Charles Simpson had one, Mr. Wallace Davis had one and Jerome Doxey had one.

Charlie Snowden also had three pound nets that Mr. Tom Brumsey fished. He set them in Goose Castle Point, east of Goose Castle Point and Bells Point. Charlie had Mr. Wilton Walker build a little tunnel boat about twenty feet long and pretty wide for Mr. Tom to fish those nets. I sat on a block of wood one day and watched Mr. Wilton plank the dead rise in the bow of that boat. Her bottom was stave planked (planked crossways). Mr. Wilton would mark a board, chop it out with a hatchet, nail it up there and caulk it.

Wharf at Currituck in the late 1800s. This is where the wharf in this story still was in the early 1900s and where the ferry dock to Knott's Island is now. *Courtesy of Henry Doxey*.

Carter Lindsey on Currituck Wharf in the fifties. The boat is Mr. Lou Brumsey's gas boat that he fished with in the winter. When I was a little boy, Daddy paid Carter five dollars to teach me how to swim. I remember sitting up on Carter's belly while he was lying back floating in the water. Carter Lindsey once worked as the "Fat Man" in "The Greatest Show on Earth." He also advertised Beautyrest mattresses at a store in Norfolk, Virginia. He'd go and stretch out on the bed in the storefront window as a model for how strong and comfortable the mattresses were. *Courtesy of Wilson Snowden.*

Amos Etheridge was a big black man who used to fish with Mr. Lou Brumsey, but later fished with Henry Doxey along with Numa Barnard. They ran the rig for about a year and a half; then Numa got a better job, and Mr. Jack Walker started fishing with Henry.

One day they went up to Tulls Bay and made two hauls in that muddy bottom and only caught about half a box of fish. They came out of the bay. It was slick calm, about two o'clock in the afternoon, and they got along there in the sound off by the Creekmoors' house. Amos was riding in the back of the skiff. Henry saw a real muddy place in the water. He pointed it out to Numa and said, "That might be fish over there. I'm going over there and see what it is."

When Henry got over there, it was nothing but solid catfish. They were boiling in there. It would be dark by five o'clock. He told Numa, "Let's stick her. We ain't gonna run out too far." He then hollered the same thing out to Amos, who replied, "Naw, Mr. Henry, I don't think so. I'm tired."

"I can't help that," said Henry. "If we can catch some fish, we got to catch 'em. That's catfish."

Bootie Spruill (seated) and Dailey Williams. This is what a "pocket of fish" looks like. *Courtesy of Susie Spruill.*

"Yeah it is, ain't it?" Amos agreed.

Henry told them he was going to get a little closer before sticking the net. They ran her around and pulled in half a box of fish in the first pocket (the section from one stick of the net to the next). They were rolling in catfish in every pocket. Before they got the net in they were about to sink the boat.

"What are we going to do?" Numa asked.

"Swing the gas boat around here," Henry said, "we're going to load her."

It was getting dark. At nearly 8:00 p.m., they were getting the last pocket of fish rolled in when the fin of a big catfish went right in the instep of Amos's foot. He screamed, "A fish is in my foot!"

"What are we gonna' do?" Numa wanted to know. Henry told him not to bend it or it might break off in there.

"Amos," Henry said, "I know it's going to hurt, but we got to pull that thing out."

"Just do sumpin'." Henry put his foot on Amos's, took hold of that catfish and gave it a snatch. Amos hollered. When the fish came out, it took a hunk of meat with it right out of his foot.

Henry Doxey teaching his son, Marvin, to mend nets. *Courtesy of Jean Doxey.*

Because it was so late, Henry knew everybody figured they were out there broke down. He looked up and saw running lights on a boat. He had an old kerosene lantern in the cabin. He lit that and set it on top of the cabin of the boat. It was Mr. Earl Snowden coming to look for them. "Are you broke down?"

"No," Henry told him, "we got a load of fish on."

Mr. Earl looked and said, "Good golly, I reckon."

By the time they got back to Currituck Wharf, it was midnight. Charlie took Amos to the doctor and he was out of work for a month.

Charlie Snowden

Charlie Snowden started a hunting lodge in the old Snowden house on Maple Road in the late thirties. The Snowdens were a prominent family in the Maple area of Currituck County. Charlie's mother, Miss Carrie, who was my wife Jo Ann's grandmother, did the cooking and housekeeping part of the lodge. It was her house. She was the matriarch of the family. Alethia Trotman helped her cook and keep house. Alethia's husband, Jimmy, had an old mule that he tended folks' gardens with and he helped around the lodge. They lived in a little house in the yard out back of the lodge.

Each guide Charlie used was responsible for his own rig. Charlie would get a truckload of juniper blocks from the shingle mill at Acorn Hill in Gates County. The men would make decoys out of them up in the Snowdens'

The Snowden family. *Front row, left to right*: Louis, Mamie, Brian, Margaret, Will Jimmy Trotman; *back row*: John, Earl, Thue, Guy and Charlie. *Courtesy of Jo Ann Morris*.

Miss Carrie Snowden, matriarch of the family pictured on the previous page and grandmother of my wife, Jo Ann. *Courtesy of Jo Ann Morris.*

backyard. Henry said that everybody who had a hand had a right (to make decoys, that is). They got a hatchet and drawknife and sharpened them as good as they could. They also used a rasp. They made a vise out of a two-by six-foot board that went from the bench to the ground to hold the duck while they were working on him.

Charlie was a fish buyer and got the hunting parties together and had several fishing rigs that he hired other people to run. During the years when we had the dog track in Moyock, Charlie was "in" with the head honchos of the track. He was like "Boss Hog" at that time in Currituck. Our phones back then were party lines and we had crank telephones. One time, Charlie was half lit and couldn't get the phone operator. He went in Taylor Brothers' store in Maple, bought an axe, went out to the road and chopped a telephone pole down. This is a story I remember. If his sister Mamie hadn't been married to Fats Blades, president of the local phone company in Elizabeth City, he would have been in big trouble.

Charlie got most of his big battery ducks from Mr. Carl Brumsey. He and his brother, Tom, had a battery rig that they market hunted with until market hunting was outlawed in 1918. Then they carried sportsmen until the battery rig was outlawed.

There was an old building between the county wharf and Johnson's wharf that the Brumseys kept their decoys in (this was about where the dock for the ferry to Knotts Island is now). After market hunting was outlawed, this old building sat there with no repair and the floor was rotten and falling in the sound. Henry said they gave Charlie the decoys and Henry and some of the other fellows were helping Charlie cut all the strings off the decoys. He said they found forty-pound battery weights and a lot of other things that had fallen in the sound.

Mr. Earl Snowden, Charlie's brother, guided at the lodge for a year or two and then he went out on his own. Dr. Fondie, from Norfolk, got Mr. Pat O'Neal to build Mr. Earl a gas boat. She was about twenty-five feet long, had a cabin on it and a Chrysler Crown Marine engine in it. This is the first boat I can remember Mr. Pat building. It was the only gas boat I knew of that had a marine engine in it, aside from the club boats. I can remember when I thought I'd never be able to own a boat that had a marine engine with a clutch in it. All the local folks had boats with old car engines that went when you hit the starter. When you wanted to stop, you cut the switch off.

Mr. Earl's deal with Dr. Fondie was that he was to take Dr. Fondie hunting when he wanted to go. All the rest of the time, he could use the boat for anything he wanted to. Mr. Earl hunted with the boat during the hunting season and fished with it the rest of the winter.

Sea Lizard

Charlie Snowden, Russell Box, Fats Blades (Charlie's brother-in-law), Charlie Kight and Henry Doxey didn't have any sportsmen one day, so they went hunting themselves. They were going to take the boat named the *Sea Lizard*. The boat didn't have a shelter cabin like it had when I later owned it.

Henry said they took one of the float boxes and just put it up on top of the cabin and tied it down because there wasn't enough room for both the box and them in the back. I still haven't figured out how they got it on top of the cabin, but Henry said they did, so I'm sure they did.

This picture was taken at Mill Landing in Maple when I owned the boat. When Charlie Snowden had it built, it just had the forward cabin. Rufus Roberts, from whom I bought it, added the shelter cabin. It was built in the yard of Rehoboth Baptist Church in 1937 by Oliver O'Neal and Carlos Culpepper. It had the widest Juniper boards on its sides I've ever seen. The old Maple Warehouse Company was just to the right of where the *Sea Lizard* is tied up. *Author's collection.*

They tied out in Belluses (that's between the Knotts Island ferry dock and Mackey Island). It is deep water—seven to nine feet. They were killing ducks, but it was cold as ice. Every drop that was flying was freezing right to the boat. The wind shifted to the northwest and they decided they had better take up. They got everything taken up and got the box on board, but then they had to tie it down. They had to beat the ice off the washboards so they could get to the bow to tie her down. Henry said he knew that was going to be his job. He told Charlie to put a rope on him because he knew he was going overboard.

Henry got back without falling overboard, but the box had slipped a little to one side. He told Charlie to pull on a rope to get her back straight. Charlie was about half lit and, about the time he pulled on that rope, the boat rolled and he went overboard, end over winding. They got Charlie back in the boat and he was about frozen.

"Throw her overboard and leave her or tie her down, but do sumpin'. I'm freezing to death," he said. They got that Model A Ford motor going and soon the manifold was cherry red. Charlie was lying right across the engine box. They had the top off it so he could get all the heat he could. They had the skiff in tow and were heading for home. It was night when they left Belluses…and it was a dark night at that.

When they got to Goose Castle Point (the north end of Church's Island), Henry told Charlie he thought he was right to go through the Haul-over (this is between what used to be Little Bells and Big Bells Island). Charlie raised up off the engine box and looked up in the sky and said, "See those two stars up there?"

Henry said, "Yeah."

"Head for them," Charlie said, "and you'll go right through the Haul-over."

Henry said he had that Model A clucking and all of a sudden BLAM, BLAM. The gas boat came up on her side and the skiff nearly turned over and threw the decoys all out the side.

"What in the hell happened?!?" Charlie asked.

"I ran through the bush blind," Henry responded.

"Where's the skiff?" Charlie asked. Henry told him it was still tied behind them. Charlie told him to pour it on her and keep going.

When they got to the dock at Mill Landing there was ice on it. Fats Blades was a big man and he was feeling no pain. When he was getting off the boat his feet slipped out from under him and he went overboard. Henry said he and Charlie Kight liked to have never pulled him back up on the dock. They loaded Fats and Charlie into Charlie Kight's 1936 Ford and carried them up to Charlie Snowden's house to dry out, in more ways than one, before Fats went home to Mamie.

Guiding for Charlie Snowden

I guided two winters in the mid-fifties for Charlie or Mr. Earl Snowden. It was Charlie's rig, but Mr. Earl paid me. Mr. Wallace Davis and I ran the rig with the old Tom Brumsey battery boat. She was thirty-two feet long.

We swam geese all day, mostly from Goose Castle north. A lot of times we'd be off Currituck Shore. At the time, the limit was two geese per man and we usually got our limit. We'd see a bunch of geese, tie the box out and swim the geese to it. This is not as simple as it sounds. If they got up, we had to take the rig up and find another bunch. Sometimes we had to do that two or three times a day. We didn't tie out many ducks; these men mainly wanted to hunt geese. I think most of them were from Ohio. When we got our limit, we could come in. Swimming geese wasn't legal, but everybody did it.

The other rig Charlie had when I was guiding for him was a big old thirty-two-foot battery boat that had belonged to Bells Island Club. In fact, it was the boat I made my first duck hunting trip in when I was six years old. Mr. Clara Doxey ran that rig for Charlie with help from Pudding Rawls. Their box was heavier than ours and that boat had the same old mast, with blocks and tackles that were used on the old batteries. If Pudding couldn't go, Mr. Clara wouldn't go unless I'd go with him because I knew how to handle the block and tackles. In that case, they would find somebody else to go with Mr. Wallace. We pulled our box across the skiff on that rig.

I remember one day it was frozen up so we couldn't get out to hunt. The sportsmen hired me to drive them around the county. They were about half lit and wanted me to stop down there in Harbinger where Mr. Owens had some geese fenced up. They wanted to shoot one. Needless to say, I wasn't about to do that. They paid me twenty dollars that day, which was twice what I was getting paid to guide. I was happy to drive them around.

The Monkey Island battery boat. This boat was built for Monkey Island Club by Otis Doe of Wanchese in 1910. It was donated to the Whalehead Preservation Trust by Levy Bunch Jr. It is now in the process of being restored. *Author's collection.*

Archie Midgett

Archie Midgett was a native of Coinjock. After he retired as an engineer on a tugboat with Curtis Bay Towing in Baltimore, Maryland, he came back to Coinjock and lived with Mr. Pat and Miss Madeline O'Neal. He was a cousin of Miss Madeline's. He was a bachelor and set in his ways, to say the least.

Archie got Mr. Pat to build him two big flat-bottom skiffs. He put a motor in one for a gas boat and the other one he used for a fishing skiff. A lot of afternoons after I got off work at Mr. Pat's boatbuilding shop (my first job), Archie and I and whoever else we could find would take that gas boat and go across the sound to Parker's or Ship's Bay and go mullet fishing.

In the fifties, Mr. Wallace Davis, Bill Snowden and I fished one of Archie's rigs one winter. Mr. Wallace was captain, Bill pulled the cork line and I pulled the lead line. Archie was always messing with the net and I know it wasn't fishing the bottom. I know this because other fishermen around us were catching fish and sometimes we had to take money out of our pockets to pay the gas bill. Mr. Wallace in previous years had a fishing rig of his own, and I know he was a good captain.

Some other local men who fished commercially were Mr. Van Griggs (who was referred to earlier as the holder of the record for killing the most ducks in Currituck Sound in one day) and Mr. Will Palmer. Both Mr. Will and Mr. Van had flat-bottom open gas boats with Model A Ford motors. They both kept them under the old bridge at Coinjock. That was a built-in boathouse. These men fished fike nets (kind of like a trap) in the North River. Bill Barrington, who lived on my grandmother's farm, fished with Mr. Palmer. Bill always kept us in bass and round robins. They couldn't sell them because they were classed as sport fish. I'm sure Granny gave him something for them, though.

Above: First Coinjock bridge, looking south. The Bray house and store is in the background. *Courtesy of Kevin Doxey.*

Right: Bill and Jessie Barrington. They lived on my grandmother's farm all their lives. Jessie helped with the washing and housework and later looked after my children and my oldest granddaughter, Cameron. When I was little, I used to ride with Bill in a horse cart to Coinjock to haul watermelons to load on the watermelon boats. *Author's collection.*

Ambrose "Hambone" Twiford

Ambrose Twiford, hereafter referred to as Hambone, was a legend. Mr. Pat O'Neal gave him his nickname after a cartoon in the *Progressive Farmer* called "Hambone Says." Ambrose was always hanging around in Mr. Pat's shop quoting Hambone; thus the nickname.

Hambone didn't finish high school, but he had a doctorate on Currituck Sound. He knew it better than anybody I've ever known, without exception.

When we were going to school, Hambone and I were the first ones on the school bus. He was several years older than me, but we were always good friends. I don't remember what year he quit school. His daddy died when he was young and that may have been when he quit.

Hambone on a load of sedge when we were building blinds at Monkey Island. *Author's collection.*

Hambone "turtling." *Courtesy of Susie Mae Twiford.*

Hambone started out with some turtle traps and fished with other people who had long nets. He didn't have a rig of his own then. He would like to have had his own rig, but he didn't have the money. He fished mostly out of Poplar Branch and sometimes with Henry Doxey out of Currituck Village. Hambone ran one of Archie Midgett's rigs out of Coinjock. When Archie died, he left that rig to Hambone. That's how he got started with his own rig.

Hambone poled sport fishermen around in the summer. In the winter, he fished and guided hunters. He fished mostly after the hunting season was over.

Hambone helped me take sportsmen in my float box before I ran Monkey Island and also when I ran Monkey Island from 1974 to 1978. I couldn't

The *Corolla Express* and the *Rhonda* (blue gas boat with cabin) tied up at Casey Jones's dock. *Author's collection.*

have operated it without him. He brought the guides from the mainland every morning in my gas boat, *Rhonda*. I didn't have to worry about them getting there, regardless of weather. I knew he'd have them there. He was also the best guide I ever had to help me with the float box.

One thing Hambone couldn't stand was to stay still in a blind with men all day. One time he had two men tied out at Ware Point, which is a Monkey Island blind over on Currituck Beach. It was a slick, calm day. Hambone could hear those trawlers fishing out in the ocean. He left the men in the blind, poled the skiff down the shore a ways and walked over to look at those trawlers. When he walked back, it took him a while to find where he had left his skiff.

We always took the men back to the lodge for lunch at Monkey Island. By the time Hambone found his skiff and got back to his men, it was past lunchtime. The men had killed several pintails and had to watch them drift off. When they got in, the men were fit to be tied. One of them was a lawyer from Connecticut and the other had a seat on the New York Stock Exchange. They wanted me to fire Hambone. I knew how they felt, but there was no way I was going to fire him. That just wasn't going to happen. I

Casey Jones's store at Waterlily in 1958. This is at his dock, where I kept my boats and the Monkey Island boat. *Courtesy of Faye Hooper.*

Monkey Island as viewed from the east in the seventies. *Author's collection.*

Left to right: Jimmy Markert, Fred Dunstan, Don Bullock Jr. and Travis Morris. The North Carolina Wildlife Resources Commission (WRC) had a movie made entitled *The Rhythms of Currituck*. It's about hunting and fishing in Currituck like it used to be. The movie runs every thirty minutes in the WRC in Corolla. To make the hunting part, I agreed to rig up

my old float rig, which is the closest thing to the old battery rig that is legal. They dressed us up like people would have been dressed in the twenties. In this picture, I have my glasses on, but I had to take them off in the movie; there was no plastic then. Kim DeCosta was the director and she did a great job, as I'm sure anybody that sees the movie will agree. We let the film crew stay at Piney Island and all had a great time. *Author's collection.*

Jones's Dock in Waterlily. Film crew is at the stern of the skiff; Jimmy Markert is at the skiff's bow; Fred Dunstan, Travis Morris and Don Bullock Jr. are in the *Mother Goose*. *Author's collection.*

told them I'd give them their money back and I'd take them to the mainland right then. They calmed down and had a good time.

In later years, Hambone started making decoys. They were nothing fancy. They were working decoys. He didn't like to paint his decoys, but sometimes you could get him to.

Hambone was a very shy person. He didn't like to have his picture taken. When the Wildlife Resources Commission, hereafter referred to as WRC, was going to make a movie about hunting and fishing in Currituck like it used to be, they asked me to fix up my old float rig. Hambone helped me put new bags on the box wings and get everything ready. When it came time for the filming, he said he didn't feel good and wouldn't help me. I recruited Jimmy Markert, the caretaker at Piney Island Club. They dressed us up like we would have been dressed in the twenties. They wouldn't let me wear my glasses because they said they didn't have plastic glasses in the twenties. Making the movie was fun. I got Don Bullock Jr. and Fred Dunstan to be sportsmen.

Hambone was also supposed to be the one in the movie making duck decoys. He wouldn't do that either. They had to get somebody else. The movie runs every thirty minutes in the WRC Center in Corolla. In the peak of the season, they will have 1,500 to 1,800 people a day go through the center.

Jimmy Markert has made three nice wood benches and put them on the deck of the WRC building with a plaque remembering each of the three decoy carvers on Waterlily: Ned Burgess, Bob Morse and Ambrose Twiford, "Hambone."

When the Coast Guard Wouldn't Go

When I was running Monkey Island, I kept a sixteen-foot sailboat over there for the kids to use. One fall day, my son, Walton, took some of his friends over to the island in the *Corolla Express*, an open gas boat. Ruth and Wayne, my two oldest daughters, were with them. In the afternoon, Walt took the crowd back to the mainland at Casey's Dock. Then he, Donna Williams, Lynn Sawyer and Norman Tadlock decided to go back to Monkey Island and go sailing. Late in the afternoon a storm blew up. I didn't know they were out in the sailboat. Just before nightfall, the caretaker who lived on Monkey Island at the time, John LaRoke, called me and said the kids were out in the sailboat and he didn't know where they were. To say the least,

The sailboat and some of the kids Hambone and I were looking for on that dark stormy night on Currituck Sound. *Author's collection.*

Hambone in his landing house shop where he made decoys and kept his nets. *Author's collection.*

I was upset that he had waited so late to call me. The wind was blowing at least twenty-five or thirty miles per hour. It must have been from the southwest because the tide was real high.

I went and got Hambone. He never hesitated a minute to go with me. Frances called the Coast Guard. By then, it was dark. Hambone and I went to Monkey Island. Then we went up north around Lungreen Island and worked our way all around the shore on the beach side, shining a strong spotlight I had on the *Rhonda*.

I knew if that boat turned over I'd never see them again because they couldn't hang on to it. When we got around by Raccoon Island, I was shining the light out in the sound toward some of the duck blinds. They had gotten in Roland Twiford's duck blind. They knew I couldn't see them because the boat was in the skiff way (where the hunting skiff is hidden in a duck blind). They let the line out so the boat would go about halfway out of the skiff way. When the light picked up that white boat, nobody will ever know the relief I felt.

We went to the blind. They got in the sailboat and let her back so we could get them in the *Rhonda*. They were about to freeze. They all had bathing suits on. They had put life preservers on to try to keep from freezing. We got them in the cabin of the *Rhonda* and took the sailboat in tow, then headed for Monkey Island. The mast had broken and they managed to get to that duck blind, which was the smartest thing they could have done. When we got to Monkey Island dock, the Coast Guard boys were tied up there. They said it was too rough to go out. They were going to wait until the next morning.

We secured the sailboat and took the kids back to Waterlily. I don't remember, but I think the Coast Guard boys spent the night at Monkey Island. Thus, a happy ending.

Hambone never hesitated to go with me to look for anybody overdue in the sound, no matter how bad the weather. Hambone and I have been in Currituck Sound together some mighty rough times, both day and night.

Julian "Grissie" Barco's Amazing Feat

When I knew Mr. Grissie, he had "set nets" and a little round stern gas boat. He also had a railway where he pulled up gas boats and worked on them.

Grissie told me one time that he was living in Corolla in a little house on Spry Creek that belonged to Mr. Tilman Lewark. He made a deal with Mr. Lewark for the house and took it apart. He didn't have a gas boat; just a skiff. On calm days, he would load that skiff up with boards from his house and pole it four miles across Currituck Sound to Waterlily, where he had a piece of land on the sound, and put the house back together. (Before I wrote this, I called his daughter, Faye Hooper, to be sure I understood him correctly about poling across the sound. She assured me that was right. She said sometimes somebody with a gas boat would see him and give him a tow.) I was talking to him one day and he told me a person can do anything at all. "There's nothing to it," he said, "even if it's going to the moon, as long as you thoroughly understand it." He obviously believed what he said. I've quoted him many times in that saying.

Julian "Grissie" Barco. *Courtesy of Faye Hooper.*

Grissie Barco with his daughter, Faye (now Faye Hooper), in 1937, walking up the road from the county dock in Corolla. The gate in the background went to the Whalehead Club. The lighthouse would be on the left. *Courtesy of Faye Hooper.*

Monkey Island boat on Grissie Barco's railway in the early fifties. This boat was built by Bob Morse, who was a well-known decoy carver from Church's Island (also known as "Waterlily"). *Courtesy of Faye Hooper.*

Julian "Grissie" Barco's Amazing Feat

Grissie Barco building a skiff for his grandson, Carl Hooper. *Courtesy of Faye Hooper.*

Adventures of the Pilmoor Boy Scouts in Corolla and New York

In the mid-forties, Boy Scout Troop 172, sponsored by Pilmoor Memorial United Methodist Church, was given a free week in Corolla as guests of Mr. Ray Adams, owner of the Whalehead Club. This came about because of my daddy's friendship with Mr. Adams.

Mr. Adams had bought the decommissioned Currituck Beach Coast Guard Station from the government. This station was the only thing out on the beach in Corolla at the time. As far as the eye could see, there was nothing but white sand, golden sea oats, the blue ocean and sky. Because of his good relationship with the Coast Guard, Mr. Adams got four Coast Guard boys from Caffey's Inlet Station to go up to Currituck Beach and cook for and kindly look out for the Scouts.

Mr. Earl Snowden took us from the mainland wharf at Currituck to Corolla. At the time, his brother, Charlie, owned the old thirty-two-foot Tom Brumsey battery boat. I don't mean it was powered by a battery. I mean it was built to carry a battery (or sink) box, back in the days when hunting from a sink box was legal. Charlie had somebody run it for a long-net fishing rig. A six-cylinder Chevrolet, hooked up straight (no transmission; when it was started, it moved), powered it. I can't remember how many of us there were on this trip, but there was a boatload.

We docked at Whalehead's boat basin and then our gear was carried to the beach in one of those old army trucks that Mr. Adams had. We settled in at the Coast Guard station for a week we would all remember.

We slept in a big dormitory room on the second floor. Some of the boys had to get up during the night to pee, but instead of going downstairs to the bathroom, they just peed out the windows. The next morning we realized it went into a gutter that poured into a cistern and that was where our drinking water came from. That ended peeing out the windows.

The highlight of our day was to visit Mr. Johnnie Austin's little store inside the Corolla Post Office. He opened his store for a few hours every day when the mail boat came from Waterlily. We made it a point to be at the store on time to buy candy and pick up mail from home. I met Mr. Johnnie's

Mr. Adams, Daddy and cook from Caffey's Inlet Coast Guard Station. *Author's collection.*

son, Norris, there. He was younger than we were, but Norris and I have been friends ever since that time.

On one of our trips to the store, we found some quicksand and discovered that we could work our way down in it waist deep. We elected Charles Wayne Tucker and Dukie Davis to sink into the sand after the rest of us ran to alarm the adults. After we told them, some of us ran back ahead of the adults and motioned to the two boys to jump in the quicksand. Those old men were running across those sand hills with their tongues hanging out. It's a miracle they didn't have heart attacks. When they found out what the deal was, we were well reprimanded for that prank!

Durwood Miller and Jim Quidley are the two Coast Guard boys whose names I remember. They helped us put to sea and set a net from a dory that

Boy Scout Troop 172 at Currituck beach as guests of Mr. Ray Adams, thanks to Daddy. *Author's collection.*

Scouts pile on Mr. Adams's Jeep. I'm in the front row with cap and sunglasses on. Dodson Mathias is to my left. Baxter Williams and "Tinks" (Edward Ferebee) are on the hood. Daddy is in the back row, wearing a hat. *Author's collection.*

Corolla Post Office and Mr. Johnnie Austin's store in 1947. *Author's collection.*

Mr. Adams had. After the net set a while, we'd haul it on the beach and cook our fish for supper. We enjoyed fabulous food that entire week. Mr. Adams had provided plenty of meat for those Coast Guard boys to cook and we Scouts could sure eat it. It was a week we'll always remember.

When we were growing up in Currituck, there was nothing to do here. There was no television and the nearest movie theater was twenty miles away in Elizabeth City. Thursday night Boy Scout meetings gave us something to do, as did our camping trips. It is worth noting that nine of us, including Mr. Tucker, made Eagle Scout in June of 1948. The other eight were Charles Wayne Tucker, Dodson Mathias, Baxter Williams, Dukie Davis, Fletcher Humphries, Montel Cartwright, Wayne Taylor and me. At the time, that number represented the largest number of Scouts who made Eagle at one time in the Tidewater Council, perhaps even on the East Coast.

When we all made Eagle, Pilmoor Memorial Methodist Church gave us a week in New York City. It was a trip we will never forget. Daddy and Mr. Tucker, our Scoutmaster, carried us up in two cars. The Elizabeth City Band played there for the Kiwanis Parade that week, and we were lucky enough to follow around on their coattails.

We climbed to the top of the Empire State Building, went to Rockefeller Center, saw Perry Como at Madison Square Garden, boated around

Eagle Scouts: *front row, left to right*: Fletcher Humphries, Montel Cartwright, Baxter Williams and Scout Master Mr. Joe Tucker; *back row*: Charles Wayne Tucker, Wayne Taylor, Wallace "Dukie" Davis Jr., Travis Morris and Dodson Mathias. *Author's collection.*

Eagle Scouts at Piney Island for their fiftieth anniversary reunion. *Front row, left to right*: Baxter Williams, Montel Cartwright, Fletcher Humphries; *back row*: Wayne Taylor, Dukie Davis, Charles Wayne Tucker, Dodson Mathias and Travis Morris. *Author's collection.*

Manhattan Island and ate a thirteen-course meal in Chinatown. When we went to Coney Island, vendors called out for us to "Come on in, boys," and let us in everything for free. The war had just ended, and we were in our uniforms, each wearing sashes with at least twenty-one merit badges pinned on. I guess they thought we were in the army.

Another highlight was when one of our Eagles, Wayne Taylor, who won the Fisher Body Contest with his model car, was on television. The band had invited the rest of us to watch from one of their rooms at the Waldorf as he appeared on a nine-inch, black-and-white screen. It was the first television we had ever seen.

A Couple of Trips During My Coast Guard Years—1951 to 1954

In January 1951, Dodson Mathias, Baxter Williams, Edward Vance Ferebee, Wayne Taylor and I all joined the Coast Guard. After boot camp, Dodson was sent to the district office in Norfolk, as was Edward Vance. They stayed there the whole three years. Wayne and Baxter got the weather patrol cutter *Chincoteague* out of Norfolk. Later, Baxter got the district office and Wayne went to the Loran station at Hatteras. I went to the air station in Elizabeth City and they put me on the boat dock. That is where I met Herbert Lange and we have been the best of friends ever since.

We had good duty, with forty-eight hours on, forty-eight hours off and seventy-two hours off every other weekend. When we were off duty, Lange, who was from Brandywine, Maryland, always stayed at our house.

Herbert Lange with our day's kill (one blue peter) at Mill Landing in 1952. *Author's collection.*

The white boat is the one Dodson Mathias and I bought from Gilman Brumsey for thirty-five dollars. We got Mr. Wilton Walker to fix it up, put a cabin on it and a Model A Ford motor in it. It is pictured at Mill Landing, right beside where the Currituck Sports II store is today. *Author's collection.*

Dodson wanted to rig up a gas boat, so he and I bought an old boat from Mr. Gilman Brumsey for thirty-five dollars and rigged it up with a Model A Ford motor. Dodson's main objective in this was to carry his superior officers duck hunting. Dodson was looking for promotions, which he got. He was the only one of us who came out first class. Lange and I hunted many days in Coinjock Bay with that old boat. Back in those days, there were thousands

Russell Nixon and Travis Morris putting the float box over in Cedar Island Bay in 1952. *Author's collection.*

of blue peters (coot) in Coinjock Bay. You could most always kill all you wanted.

One day, Dodson and I had this officer tied in the box in Cedar Island Bay, between where I have a blind now and Oyster Cove. That afternoon, geese started coming in the bay, flying right low to the water, and I believe we killed twelve.

Another time, I had this old boat and some of Daddy's friends from Lumberton. I remember one of them was Malcolm Sewell, who later ran for governor. Anyway, it was blowing too hard for that little boat to take that big load in Currituck Sound. We got around Long Point and hadn't seen any ducks, but we saw Ambrose "Hambone" Twiford aboard the *Caroline*. Daddy hired Hambone to take us out in the sound. Then we were in the steamboat channel and the box was about to fall off that little skiff. Hambone and I got in the skiff to straighten it up and Hambone fell overboard. Now remember, this was a very cold day in December. Hambone got back in the *Caroline* and went in the cabin, where he put on a pair of oilskins and a pair of long drawers. That was all the clothes he had and he stayed out there the rest of the day. We killed several geese and Hambone killed one from the gas boat with a slug at a distance I didn't believe was possible to kill one from.

One day Dodson's daddy—Mr. Adrian Mathias—Lange and I went out with the same old boat. We tied the box out just north of Long Point and then Lange and I got in. I am a very poor shot; never could hit a thing. Mr. Adrian was running the boat and he got a bunch of geese up. They started coming to us as pretty as you have ever seen, flapping just above the water. Lange and I were down in the box just peeping. We were almost scared to breathe, afraid it would flare them. When they got in range, Lange whispered, "Take 'em," and we started shooting. Every time I pulled the trigger, a goose would fall. If I hadn't seen it, I wouldn't have believed it. Lange did the same thing. We got all six. Three more geese came to us and we got them, too. Mr. Adrian came quickly, since that was our limit and we thought we had better go.

I remember one time when wheat was planted in the field behind Mr. Adrian's house and a lot of geese were going in there. He wouldn't let anybody shoot them until Dodson got home from Wake Forest College one weekend. On the appointed day for the goose hunt, Mr. Adrian called and invited me to come up and join him and Dodson. Needless to say, I was very excited because I had been watching those geese go in the field every day. I got to their house early on Saturday morning. I had my old Model 11 Remington and Mr. Adrian and Dodson each had a double-barrel gun (Mr. Adrian did a lot of quail hunting).

It was a clear, cold, frosty morning. We walked to the back of the field and got in a ditch where the geese had been going. We hadn't been there long before we heard the geese honking. As the honking got closer, we were still as mice, afraid to even blink an eye. They circled around a time or two and then lit about thirty feet from the ditch. The only problem was, they were about two hundred feet down the ditch from where we were! Well, it was a shallow ditch and there was a little water in it, but there was only one thing to do. We crawled and slid along on our bellies until we got right off against those geese. Mr. Adrian gave the word, and we jumped up and cut loose, emptying all our guns. When the smoke had cleared, we looked around and all we had was a goose with a broken wing that was running across the field. Dodson and I took out after him with Mr. Adrian hollering, "Catch him, boys!" We finally ran the old goose down, carried him to the house and chopped his head off with an axe.

A Page from the Past

H ere is a page from the log book of the "Roving Hunters," November 25, 1967, that shows how I've kept my logs over the years:

Date: November 25, 1967
Wind: West, about 15 mph; dying to dead calm about noon
Sky: Overcast, changing to sunny with haze about noon
Temperature: Mild
Rig: Laydown box
Location: Out from Brock's Bay on edge of the shoal between Mark Doxey's blind and Robert's Brothers' blind
Hunters: Vernon Lee Creekmore, Gordon Sawyer, Baxter Williams, Walton Morris, Travis Morris
Game: 1 Canvasback; 4 Widgeon; 10 Redheads

Baxter and Gordon were pushing the box off the skiff and Baxter fell overboard. I gave him some of my clothes and he didn't fare too bad.

I let Walton take my old Model 11 Remington automatic for the first time today. We had no more than anchored the boat when I looked back and a bunch of ducks were going to him. He knocked out two. Before we could pull the anchor, he had knocked out another. He had one dead and two cripples, which we lost. Ducks were flying too fast for me to stay there and look around. He killed two more dead.

Needless to say, this ranks among my greatest hunting days, to see my son do something I've never been able to do, but if we both live and nothing happens I'll give him the chance to pull up on many a Canvasback and Redhead.

I had rather teach my son to appreciate and feel the true beauty of Canvasback on a still afternoon, and the silver wings of Swan over the sand dunes against a sea blue sky, than to teach him to love a dollar so well he can't take the time to absorb what nature has endowed Currituck with so bountifully.

My son, Walton, at our house in Currituck in 1973. The last afternoon of the duck season, Mr. Carl White invited Mr. Kenyon Wilson and my son to hunt at Pine Island. Mr. Wilson was living in Corolla at the time. Walt took my gas boat *Rhonda* to Corolla. I waited for him to get back across the sound that night at Jones's dock. He was young and by himself. *Author's collection.*

His Granny (my grandmother), who is 93, told me tonight she felt sure he would be a duck hunter like his ancestors who have lived in Currituck for about the last 200 years.

Big Fish

In February of 1968, Jimmy Hayman, Newton Hampton and Graham Keaton caught the largest fish that I've ever heard of being caught in Currituck Sound. They were fishing Casey Jones's haul seine fishing rig.

The fish was a 231-pound sturgeon. It was 7½ feet long and had a 4-foot-long roe. Sturgeon normally inhabit northern Atlantic waters. They live in the ocean, but migrate into fresh water to spawn. I have heard of sturgeon being caught in Currituck Sound, but never one that big. The men finally got the bowline of the fishing skiff, which was a long line, around the tail of the fish. They said if he got away, at least he'd take them with him. It took them about thirty minutes, but they finally got him in the boat.

Newton Hampton told me that Mr. Casey Jones carried the fish to Globe Fish Company in Elizabeth City, which, in turn, shipped it to Fulton Fish Market in New York City. Newton said they had to wait a few days to get their money and, when they did get it, it was less than one hundred dollars. He said they told them it was not the right kind of roe. At any rate, it was a big fish, and for a little while they thought they had really made some money.

Left to right: Newton Hampton, Graham Keaton and Jimmy Hayman with "the Big Fish," a sturgeon caught in Currituck Sound. *Courtesy of Jo Ann Morris.*

Sketches of Growing Up in Currituck

Before telling more "modern" fishing and hunting tales (1980s and beyond), I'm going to share some brief memories that just came to mind about growing up in Currituck.

The first road I remember through here was a sixteen-foot-wide cement road. One time I was riding my bicycle to Mr. Caleb Cayton's store, and there was a place where the cement was about two inches higher than the shoulder. I ran off the road, and when I pulled back on, she threw me. It looked like someone had taken a spoon and scooped out my right elbow. Mama carried me to Dr. Griggs and he put some black stuff on it that looked like tar. That scar will go with me to my grave.

While speaking of Dr. Griggs, I think it might be interesting to note that when I was growing up, if anybody needed Dr. Griggs, they would stick a pitchfork in the ground out by the road and hang a white towel on it. If you wanted Dr. Mann, who lived in Moyock in the north end of the county, you hung a red towel on the pitchfork. Anybody who saw either of these would tell them where they were needed. I might add that they didn't want to know if you had the money to pay them before they came to see you.

Dr. Griggs lived in Poplar Branch and was never married. I have heard people who lived in Corolla say that if somebody there was sick or having a baby, they went to get him anytime of the day or night. If it was cold weather, he'd take a blanket to wrap up in. He'd get up in the bow in the boat under the spray hood or cabin (if the boat had one) and sleep while crossing the sound.

In 1939, people in the county took up a collection and bought Dr. Griggs a new 1939 Ford Coupe.

I had a billy goat that Daddy bought for me from some boys in Gates County for five dollars. They had trained him to drive like a mule. I had a harness for him and a four-wheel wagon with a seat on it just like a regular farm wagon that I got for Christmas one year. I drove the old goat to Mr. Cayton's store many times. Sometimes the goat would pull my socks off the clothesline and eat them, which made Mama quite angry.

My granny, Carrie Boswood, and me with my billy goat, "Bill," and the cart I got one Christmas. *Author's collection.*

Ferry across Coinjock Canal in 1920. The guardhouse and store are in the background. *Courtesy of Kevin Doxey.*

Watermelon boats loading at Coinjock. My mother, Edna Boswood Morris, took this picture in 1931. *Author's collection.*

The first movie I ever saw was on a barge, the Adams Floating Theatre, that was tied up south of the old Coinjock bridge. My Granddaddy and Grandmother Boswood carried me to see it. It was a silent movie.

Along this same area of the canal bank, there would be watermelon boats lined up in the summertime. These were Chesapeake Bay oyster buy boats that didn't have anything to do in the summer and would come here and haul watermelons to Light Street in Baltimore, Maryland. I can remember hauling watermelons to these boats in a horse cart with Bill Barrington, who worked on my grandparents' farm.

The nearest point a train came to Coinjock was between Snowden Station and Shawboro. The old folks used to say that when you could hear the train blowing, it was going to rain. That is still a pretty good sign.

I guess it was along the canal bank where Bill Tate's house is now that Mr. George Meiggs had a steam sawmill. It later belonged to Mr. Gaither Bright. Our house was about a mile from the mill, but you could hear that old whistle very plain. When she blew for noon, all the field hands knew it was dinnertime. Then she would blow again at 1:00 p.m. to go back to work.

World War II

I remember they used Daddy's office at Currituck for a plane watch station. They sent a sheet out with silhouettes of all the different types of aircraft. Volunteers stayed on watch twenty-four hours a day, and every time a plane would go over they had to call in and report it. The phone Daddy had then was one you had to crank.

In the summer of 1942, Daddy was searching the title to a large tract of land in Dare County for Mr. Harry A. Julian. I remember the name because, at the time, he was secretary of the U.S. Treasury and his name was on dollar bills. This was going to take about a month, so Daddy decided that he and Mama and I should spend that month at the First Colony Inn Hotel in Nags Head. It was during the time that the German submarines were sinking our ships. Everyone had to have dark green shades over the windows that were facing the ocean so that no light showed through. Cars had to have the top half of the headlights painted black; you only drove at night when necessary. I remember one night we saw three tankers burning offshore.

The army had long convoys that went by our home; they were going to the beach on maneuvers.

When we went to the store, we had to have ration coupons to buy groceries, shoes, gas, tires, etc. Of course, this was the same all over the country.

I remember the blimps from the naval air station in Weeksville, North Carolina; how they used to go over our house every day on their way to the ocean for submarine patrol. Our house must have been right in the path between the blimp base and Corolla lighthouse.

During this time, the government built an emergency landing strip at Maple. Due to this, Currituck County has a good four-thousand-foot runway (extended in recent years to seven thousand feet).

Uncle Ed McHorney

Uncle Ed was my granny's brother. He died in 1964, when he was eighty-six. He never married and lived in the house next door to Granny; this was the house they were both born in. The house was never plumbed or wired.

The only car Uncle Ed ever had was a 1931 Pontiac Coupe that he always parked in the buggy shed; he wrapped up the hood with a quilt in the wintertime.

He had a little woodstove in the kitchen that he cooked breakfast on. He sat in there during the morning. In the afternoon, he built a fire in the fireplace in the living room and sat in there until bedtime.

Uncle Ed McHorney and his 1931 Pontiac Coupe. *Author's collection.*

Uncle Ed would borrow my Granddaddy Boswood's mule, which was all right until one day when my Granddaddy Boswood wanted to borrow Uncle Ed's mule and he wouldn't let him. They fell out. This is the way things were as far back as I can remember. After that, Granny would walk over to Uncle Ed's every day and take him his midday meal. If it was raining, Pop would take her in the car up to the front gate. Pop died May 14, 1941, and Gladstone (Daddy's brother) was standing out in the backyard when he saw Uncle Ed coming across the field.

"I God, Gladstone, is it really so? Is he really dead?" Uncle Ed asked.

"Yes, Mr. McHorney, he is dead," replied Gladstone. From that day forward as long as Uncle Ed lived, he came over to our house every day and ate dinner. Then he would go to Coinjock to get the mail and to the store for what groceries Granny wanted.

One day—this was probably in the forties and we didn't have much traffic then—Uncle Ed was turning in to his house and a car from New York ran into him, but didn't do much damage. He got out and said, "I God, man, didn't you know I lived here?!?" In later years, I asked him if that was so. He said he guessed it was; they told it on him anyway. I never saw him look in the mirror in his car. He always cranked his head around and looked out the back window and never gave a signal.

I remember one day Uncle Ed came over home with the mule, Carrie, and cart. I don't remember why he drove the mule, because he usually came in his car. I can see him right now. He had on a black vest and suit coat. The coat was not buttoned. He started home and Carrie the mule heard those cart boards flapping and ran away. Uncle Ed was hollering, "Whoa, Carrie, WHOA!!" but Carrie was going home at full speed.

One more tale I remember about Uncle Ed. The starter in the Pontiac was in the floor. You mashed the starter with your foot to start it. The gearshift was also in the floor. Uncle Ed would get in the Pontiac, wiggle the gearshift lever (didn't push the clutch in) and jam his foot down on the starter. When he wasn't looking, I'd slip her in reverse. When he jammed down on the starter, she'd go backwards He would say, "I God, every time I get in her, she wants to go backward. I got to take her to Marcus." Marcus Griggs was the local mechanic. I decided I better leave it alone.

When I was farming, I rented a lot of land, including Granny's and Uncle Ed's. I plowed that ground many days and thought about my ancestors who had plowed the same ground with horses and mules. When I would be plowing in the fall and spring, I loved to smell the aroma of burning oak wood coming from the chimney of Uncle Ed's house.

Uncle Ed could tell me just how many rows I could go up the hill on that land from the ditch that would grow good potatoes and cabbage. He grew good watermelons and taught me how to grow them. When he was farming, he would sell his watermelons to the captain of a watermelon boat and then sometimes go on the boat to Light Street in Baltimore to the market where the boat was going. He may have been looking for other things on Light Street, too. After the boat was unloaded, they would return to Coinjock for another load.

Piney Island Tales: "Cow Patrol"

An incident happened at Piney Island on Saturday, January 9, 1988, that I think is worth recording in the log.

This was a cold day, with the temperature just above freezing. After breakfast, Fred Dunstan, Dewitt McCotter, Don Bullock and I were sitting at the game table going over the proposed budget for 1988. We had a nice fire roaring in the fireplace and it was cozy in the clubroom. DeWitt and Fred were planning to go back to Rocky Mount shortly, but they were getting drowsy and talked of taking a nap before heading out. About this time, somebody glanced out the window and saw bunch after bunch of ducks falling into the ponds on Piney Island Boulevard.

This brought everybody to attention! DeWitt jumped up and went to the window by the bar for a better look, after which he immediately took off for the phone at the south end of the hall to call his wife, Denny. He came back all smiles. She had given him permission to stay until about 4:30 p.m.

Now, Fred took off down the hall to call Dianne, but he came back with a long face. It seems that they were supposed to catch a plane to New York at 7:00 p.m. and if he didn't get home Dianne was not going to be happy with him (to put it mildly).

I told DeWitt I would go with him, so while he took his nap, I went home to get my boots and gun. I guess I got back about 2:30 and DeWitt was ready. Norman had just come to feed up. We told him where we were going so he wouldn't shower us with corn.

We got in my old yellow Jeep and drove to the pond. The place was loaded with mallards, teal and wood ducks. They, of course, flew out. We got our guns and headed for the blind in a hurry. We hadn't been in there long when they started to come back. They were in big bunches and you could hear the wind come from their wings when they would come over and then circle again.

We didn't want to shoot the big bunches, but there was one single that came by pretty close. DeWitt said if that bastard came back, he was going to shoot him.

The yellow Jeep DeWitt McCotter and I were driving the day of the "Cow Patrol." Note the piece of wood on the cement in front of the house. This is a rib out of the shipwreck *Metropolis*. This ship wrecked on Currituck Beach in 1876, with a loss of ninety-three lives. *Author's collection.*

About that time, we looked up and the sky was full of ducks, but there was also an airplane circling us. We figured that must be the game warden. We got down in the bottom of the blind and hid our faces. He kept circling the island and coming over us. We knew he saw Norman up on the north end with the tractor putting out corn.

DeWitt said, "Let's get the hell out of here," and he was halfway to the Jeep before I could even get out of the blind! This all took place in about fifteen minutes. I carried him back to the clubhouse and then I headed on home. When I got out on Church's Island Road, the plane circled over toward me. I said to myself, "He sees this yellow Jeep that left the pond so quick and knows something must be going on."

I went on home and my granddaughter was spending the night with us. I was telling Frances about the plane and Cameron said, "Granddaddy, that plane was looking for two 4-H Club steers that got out." She described the plane to me and it fit. It seems that the week before, two steers that Lindsey Hampton and another youngster were going to raise and show had gotten out and went into the woods. They could not find them so they had a plane get in on the search.

When DeWitt arrived in Rocky Mount, I called and told him what had happened. I told him, "It looks like we are not meant to hunt together." The last time we had tried, the outboard motor wouldn't run. That's duck hunting!

Second Day of the Long Duck Season

The hunters at Piney Island on December 29, 1992, were DeWitt McCotter, Clint McCotter and me. I had arrived at the club at 5:45 a.m. and everybody except my partners was hustling and bustling around, preparing to go hunting. It was foggy and raining. My crew members were sitting back in their drawers drinking coffee. I thought to myself, "Well, I've got it made this rainy morning. They are going to want to tie out right here by this fireplace."

My dreams were soon shattered. Bill Woltz, who only gets to come about once a year, walked inside the clubhouse and said he was the odd-numbered man, so he had no one to hunt with. Before I could open my mouth, McCotter offered, "You go with Travis and Clint. I'll stay here." Since Bill doesn't get to go often, I knew I had to get my ass out there in that rain. Don't misunderstand me. Bill Woltz is a nice guy, a good shot and a pleasure

The *Go-Devil. Author's collection.*

to be around, but I didn't want to be around anybody in that rain. I got McCotter off to himself and whispered in his ear that I'd get even with him for that.

I went out to put my rain gear on. After I got decked out in all that mess, I looked for Jimmy to ask where the *Go-Devil* keys were located. I found him already warming up his boat engine. He offered to take Bill, who walked up about that time. I told him that Jimmy would take him. I said that was better for him than going to the Mirey Pond with me. I felt relieved and thought to myself, "Now I can go back inside the warm clubhouse and stay out of this rain like a sensible person."

I turned around and there was McCotter, standing in the drizzle with just his insulated underwear on. He asked, "What's happening?" After I explained, he suggested, "We should go to the Mirey Pond just as well, shouldn't we?" My feathers fell, but I said, "If you want to." McCotter, Clint and I walked to the gunroom so they could put on their rain gear. I then stated that it didn't make sense. We were three supposedly intelligent men, sitting there getting ready to do something none of us really wanted to do. We would have rather gone upstairs by the fire, but we were going to sit out in rain and fog. They agreed, but we went anyway.

We drove Jimmy's truck down to the end of the road where the *Go-Devil* sat in the ditch all ready to ride. We unlocked the gate and went over to the boat. Clint was getting ready to throw our gear in the bottom of the boat when I said, "Whoa, Clint." With all the rain, I knew the boat had a lot of water in it. I shined the flashlight and, sure enough, there was a lot of water in it. Of course, Clint being the youngest, he was elected to bail it out. I will say this for him: he's well coordinated. He had two scoops and was bailing with both hands.

When that was done, we loaded up, turned the boat around and I gave the old *Go-Devil* a couple of pulls. We were off down the narrow, winding ditch to Mirey Pond. McCotter was in the bow holding the light and Clint was in the middle, holding on for dear life. I stood in the stern with my feet braced and ran the *Go-Devil*. Every once in a while, we hit a clump of mud and grass in the middle of the ditch. The old boat kind of rolled up on her side, but the *Go-Devil* kept on pushing her.

We soon got to Mirey Pond. Jimmy kept some stakes in there to mark a little channel, but there was one minor problem. We didn't know which side of the stakes to follow. Naturally, we picked the wrong side. When we got just about in front of the blind, the *Go-Devil* stopped. I remembered that Jimmy had said, "If you go across the pond to the mouth of the ditch, there is enough water to turn around." Now remember, we were out in the middle of a pond with one inch of water and ten feet of mud. If we couldn't get

Building duck blinds. *Author's collection.*

ourselves out, the only other way of getting out was with a Coast Guard helicopter. I said, "Well boys, if we have to wait for a helicopter, I don't know what you all are going to do, but I'm an Eagle Scout and I believe in being prepared. I've got a can of Vienna Sausage and a Diet Coke in my box." That put them to thinking. McCotter grabbed the mud stick and started shoving for all he was worth. Clint was trying to rock the boat and I revved up the *Go-Devil* for all she would do. We began to inch along. Finally, we got to the mouth of the ditch and hit enough water to turn around.

The decoys were soon tied out and we got in the blind. It stayed foggy and rained off and on. Just about the time I would shed my raincoat, there'd come a shower and I'd have to put it back on. Several bunches of teal appeared out of the fog like squadrons of jets and then flew away just as fast. McCotter managed to peel out three. Two fell in the marsh and, of course, we couldn't get to them. One fell in the water, drifted toward us and then ran aground. The wind picked up and he drifted some more. He finally floated down to us and we picked him up with a pole. The rain continued, so at 9:00 a.m. we decided it was time to head for home. When we got in, we found out that Jimmy and Bill Woltz had gotten their six ducks with five shots. And so it was on the second day of the long duck season of 1992.

The South Carolina Outlaws

(Names have been changed to protect the guilty)

The day was January 19, 1999. It was the next to last day of the duck hunting season. Two of the distinguished members of Piney Island Club, Bill and Will, were present. Remember, they are distinguished gentlemen from the Old South. They had arrived at the Currituck County Airport the day before on Bill's plane, along with his guest, Fred, and Will's son-in-law, Grant.

Will asked me the night before if Grant could hunt with David Swain, Chet (my grandson) and me. He wanted Grant to have a chance to hunt with Chet, who was ten years old and a very knowledgeable hunter for his age. He's also a good shot.

Tuesday morning came. I picked up Chet at 5:00 a.m. We stopped at Kevin's Amoco to get a "Hobo" (sausage and egg on toast). We then went on to the island, where Jimmy Markert had coffee ready and was just waking everybody up. After they all had coffee and breakfast, it was time to go to the boot room and get geared up to get out in the boats.

Bill, Will and Bill's guest, Fred, were going to Piney Cove on the north end of Piney Island. David Swain, Grant, Chet and I were going to Little Oyster Cove, which is just south of Piney Cove. Fred Dunstan, his son-in-law Ryder and Don Bullock were going to Big Oyster Cove. Chuck Wall, his son Rue and Jimmy Markert were going to Old Field Creek.

Now you have the hunting order. We all went out to our respective boats and headed out of the boat basin. It was dark except for the glow of red, green and white running lights on the boats. I was in David's boat. As soon as we were in deep water, David told us to hold on and he poured the juice to that Yamaha. The Jones brothers popped up on top and we were off up the Intracoastal Waterway. When we got to Long Point, I turned the spotlight on the pound nets so we could get around them. Then it was on to Little Oyster Cove. When we started tying out, day was just starting to break.

I handled the boat while the other boys tied out. That job was soon done, and we were in the blind. You could hear the wings of the teal going to the impoundment for breakfast, but it was still too dark to see them. David, Chet and Grant were in the box. I stayed sitting down in the skiff so I wouldn't take a chance on getting shot. Soon a teal cut by and Grant shot one time and rolled him out. Reba, the retriever, took off to get him. I said to myself, "If that boy can shoot like that, we might have a right good morning."

About that time, it looked like the Fourth of July in Big Oyster Cove. It was so dark that balls of fire were coming out of the hunters' gun barrels. I can't remember for sure, but I think all those boys over there got was one coot. The sun came up looking like a disc of fire over the horizon. I was sitting in the boat peeping through the pine bushes wishing I had a camera to capture the orange glow of that sunrise reflecting on still waters and the decoys just swinging a little on their strings in the light air.

The sun was up good and it was 8:15. The outlaws were ready for action. In the distance, I could hear the familiar call of the wild geese. It's been illegal to shoot Canada geese for several years now and they have gotten pretty tame. I didn't pay much attention to the geese. I hear them every day. In fact, the day before a bunch had lit right in the decoys with David and Chet.

The geese kept getting closer. I thought to myself, "Well, I guess that family is going over to the impoundment for breakfast."

All of a sudden it sounded like a war in Piney Cove. I turned my head just in time to see a goose falling out of the sky. I later learned that was the last of three to fall. The rest of the flock was honking in a high state of alarm. I looked all around to see if there were any blinds tied out that might have seen the crime. I didn't see any, but I'm sure the float blind tied in front of the lodge could figure out what was going on by the alarm the geese were in, but I don't think they could see them fall.

The radio was silent. David said, "I think we better let them get gone before we leave. We don't want to get mixed up with them. The game warden might be up there in the cut."

Now remember, my grandson, whom I've been trying to teach to obey the law, was watching all of this. By 8:30, we could stand it no longer and decided to take up and go back to the lodge.

When we went around the point into the sound, the outlaws had been hiding their loot and were now frantically taking up their decoys so they could get out of Dodge. Will was even taking up decoys, and he doesn't do that.

We got back to the lodge and went up to the bar for a Bloody Mary. I never heard the outlaws come in, but I heard the four-wheeler start up and saw Bill and Will speeding north with a black body bag.

My grandson, Chet Morris, seeing the South Carolina outlaws off at Currituck airport. Remember where that black bag of loot is! *Author's collection.*

Now, time was of the essence. Breakfast was to be served at 10:00 a.m. and Bill's plane was to pick them up at the Currituck Airport at 11:30. Of course, I knew there was no danger of them getting left. Soon I heard the four-wheeler flying back. Breakfast was ready. They came busting in the door and heading for their rooms to get out of their gear.

I asked Will what they did with the geese. He said they put that body bag in Chuck's Suburban and they were going to put them in the nose of that plane and take them back with them to South Carolina. He said they couldn't find but two of them and they didn't have time to look for the third one. I said, "Where is he? Jo Ann has been wanting a goose to eat." Will told me where he thought he was.

After breakfast, Chuck took the gentlemen to the airport. Don Bullock took his dog Bo and the four-wheeler and went back to the scene of the crime, where they finally found the third goose. I called Jo Ann and told her what I had. She knew what we had to do because we couldn't take him to the picker. When Don got back, he hid the goose. I told him I didn't want to know where he was until I was ready to go home.

I waited until night to leave so maybe I wouldn't be as likely to meet a warden. I stuffed him down behind the seat in Jo Ann's pickup and headed home. When I put Chet out at his house, I told him not to dare mention to any of his friends what we had done. He assured me he would not tell anybody.

After supper, Jo Ann and I got that old goose out in the garage and picked him. Then she took him in and cleaned him. He was one of the fattest geese I've ever seen. His meat was just as white as chicken. We looked forward to eating him. He had eaten a lot of Piney Island corn.

And so it was with my friends, the gentlemen outlaws from South Carolina.

Hatteras Duck Hunting Trip

In December of 1999, I got a call from Sandy Thorpe inviting me to go to Hatteras to duck hunt with him in a curtain blind. I was to go to Hatteras on January 9, 2000, and hunt on January 10 and 11.

A curtain blind is a box buried in the sand out on a shoal in Pamlico Sound. It has wings on it like an old battery box and canvas curtains to pull up to keep the seas out. You are sitting below the water. The only thing sticking out is your head. These things fill up with water and you have to pump them out when you go there to hunt. I'm sure they are just as potentially deadly as an old battery used to be.

I was looking forward to the experience and at the same time dreading it because I figured I was in for a freezing. The more I thought about it, the more I was dreading it. I could just picture us out there wet and cold and looking around seeing nothing but water as far as I could see. I decided I better start praying for warm weather, and the Man Upstairs answered that prayer.

As the appointed day got close, Sandy called and said he had talked to the guide, Ken Dempsey, and Ken told him that the high tides had floated his sink box up and the tide had been so low since then he couldn't get to it to get it back down. He said he was sure we would have good hunting in the stake blinds. Sandy said Ken told him we would need waders. I said I didn't have any waders and asked if hip boots would do. He said he'd call Ken and find out.

Sandy called back that night and said he thought I could get by with hip boots. I got to thinking about that and decided if the guide said we needed waders, I best have them. Fred Dunstan, David Swain and Jimmy Markert all offered to loan me theirs. The problem was they all wear size eleven. I tried them and couldn't get my foot in them. I called Currituck Sports but they didn't have any my size. Then I called Norman Gregory at the New Fowler Store in Elizabeth City. He had neoprene waders in my size. I was there in a few minutes to get a pair.

I called Sandy back to tell him I had the waders, and he let me know that Brent Nash and Randy Barnes were going to go with us. He said he had a

Roger Barnes, Brenda Gale Thorpe's brother. *Author's collection.*

Ken Dempsey, *top*, our guide and Brent Nash. *Author's collection.*

room reserved for each of us at the Holiday Inn in Hatteras (this was before he and Brenda had finished restoring their house there). They were going to leave Rocky Mount at noon Sunday. I was going to leave Maple at 3:00 p.m. We figured we'd all arrive around happy hour.

I packed up all my gear, everything I thought I might need, including my fishing gear, and put it in my Suburban. I got underway at 3:00 as planned, stopped at the 7-11 to buy a disposable camera and was off to the beach. It was a beautiful Sunday afternoon, but the weatherman was predicting rain and high winds for Monday. The temperature was in the sixties. Jo Ann was glad to get rid of me for a couple of days, and I was enjoying driving down to the beach by myself, listening to Patsy Cline, Jim Reeves, Boxcar Willie, Elvis and bluegrass music.

After I crossed the Herbert Bonner Bridge, I called Sandy to see where he was. He was just coming up on Hatteras Village, but had to go by the house he was restoring to drop off some paint and would probably get to the hotel the same time as I did.

I had just checked in when Sandy and Randy drove up. As soon as they checked in, Brent drove up. He had been down to the point to see if anybody was catching rockfish, but nobody was fishing. As soon as we all got straight in our rooms, Randy and I went down to Brent's room for a drink. Sandy was feeling bad. He said he was going to take a shower and lay down a few minutes. He said he had taken a bottle of Pepto Bismol on the way to Hatteras.

It was getting on about 7:00 p.m., and we decided if we wanted any supper we had better start looking for it. We first went to the deli at the ferry landing because Ken said we needed to get what food we wanted for lunch the next day. We asked the girl at the deli if she would make us some sandwiches. We had refrigerators in our rooms and thought we had better get them that night. She talked us into waiting until 5:30 Monday morning. She said they would be fresher.

We later figured out she didn't want to make them because she was getting ready to close and she wouldn't be the one on duty the next morning. We asked her where we could find a restaurant open to get supper. She suggested two. We decided we had better get with it because we were all hungry and didn't want to miss supper.

I kept driving. Sandy said, "It's just a little farther." Finally he admitted that we may have passed it. Just about that time, we saw a sign that said Soundside Restaurant. We were glad to see it was open, and I quickly pulled in.

Randy and I had Cajun tuna and Brent had marinated tuna. As much as Sandy likes spicy food, he decided he had better have flounder. This, along with Hatteras clam chowder, hit the spot. On the way back to the motel, we decided we had better get a 4:30 wake-up call, since we were supposed to meet Ken at Oden's Dock at 6:00 a.m.

We were all tired. It didn't take much TV to get us to sleep. I had laid all my clothes out the night before so that, when the wake-up call came, all I had to do was jump in them and go.

We decided to go in Brent's car because he had the third seat down and had room for more gear. He backed out and stopped. He said he better look at his tires; they didn't feel just right. He had let the air out of them when he went out on the point and hadn't pumped them back up. After he looked, all seemed to be okay.

We went to the deli. The man was very pleasant. He fixed our sandwiches. We got coffee, ham and egg and sausage and egg biscuits for breakfast. He really made good biscuits. Then we went back to the motel to suit up. When I bought those waders, Norman told me not to wear any pants with them, just long drawers. I took his advice. I've been duck hunting for sixty years and I never had any of these modern, fancy camouflage clothes like that sportswear until the past two years. I preferred to wear my old clothes like I'd always worn. Before this trip was over, I was glad for the modern clothes.

Now that we were all suited up, we headed for Brent's Suburban and Oden's Dock. Hunting here was a new experience for all of us, and we didn't know what to expect. When we got out of the Suburban, it was still pitch dark and the wind was howling. We walked over to the dock where we met our guide, Ken Dempsey, and his young helper, Rich. They showed us where the boat was docked and told us to put our gear on the dock by the boat. The boat was an open twenty-four-foot Carolina Sea Skiff with a 115-horsepower Suzuki outboard motor.

Ken said we were going to Ocracoke and, because of the shoals, we would have to wait until it began to get a little bit light. There were three other sportsmen he was taking. I think they were from around Cary, North Carolina.

After about fifteen minutes, Ken was ready to load up. Ken was just as nice as he could be. He told us to take our time and he'd help us in the boat. I was the "oldest rat in the barn," as Thad Eure (former secretary of state for North Carolina) used to say about himself, so I decided to be the first in the boat. I wanted a back seat facing the stern. I knew it would be less bumpy and I wouldn't be facing the wind. Sandy said he figured I knew something, so he followed me and we both had back seats.

With everybody loaded up, we headed out the breakwater into Pamlico Sound and then for Ocracoke at full speed in a thirty-five- to forty-mile-per-hour southwester. There were nine of us in that boat. After this trip, I have a lot of respect for the Carolina skiffs; so much, in fact, that I have since bought one.

I was immediately thankful for all that modern foul weather gear. I was toasty warm and dry, but water was hitting my back like somebody was throwing five-gallon buckets of water at me. There was a bailing scoop made from a gallon Clorox jug and every now and then I'd bail a few scoops.

As it began to get light, the sky was heavily overcast. We were now running in very shallow water, but still at full speed. Ken had tilted the motor all he could, but it was kicking a rooster tail of sand. Finally, the motor was hitting so hard he had to stop. We were probably seventy-five yards from the blind.

Here is where I learned something from Brent Nash. He had a walking stick. This can be very essential when you are walking in the water loaded down with gear and the bottom is full of holes where the ducks have been feeding. It gives you something to help you keep your balance. I also brought two seat cushions. When I loaded these, I still didn't know for sure if we were going to hunt in the sink box, but if we did, I knew it would be wet.

Now that I was out where I could look around, I saw something I haven't seen since I was a boy. There were smokes of redheads and pintails. By this I mean clouds of them. It was gratifying just to look at them and know they still existed. When I was a boy, I had seen clouds of ducks like that in Currituck Sound, but I don't think I've ever seen that many clouds of them. Of course, Currituck is just a pond compared to Pamlico Sound. Everywhere you'd look, you would see a smoke of ducks.

Since Ken could only get the boat about seventy-five yards from the blind, we had to walk the rest of the way in. Now remember, it's a southwester blowing thirty-five to forty miles per hour and it had started to rain. When we got to the blind there was a ladder to get up in it. The blind was ten feet long and four feet wide with a two-foot-wide top over the seat. It was first class. The decoys were already tied out. Brent counted 103. They were redheads, canvasback, pintail and Canada geese all mixed together.

As soon as we got settled in, we loaded up our guns. Just about that time, I heard a boom. Roger had killed a duck too far for us to walk and get. Ken later picked him up. It was really a long shot. Next, bufflehead started cutting by and the boys didn't want to shoot them. They were saving their limit for redheads and pintail. I told them they better shoot some of those buffleheads. In fact, I even killed one. I think they finally killed four.

We hunkered down under that top when the rain squalls came and took turns standing up and watching. Every time you would look up, there

Travis Morris retrieving a duck at Hatteras. *Author's collection.*

would be a smoke of redheads boiling up in the distance. That wind had them stirring. Finally, seven redheads came right up the string like they are supposed to do, and we got six of them. That's the way duck hunting in Currituck used to be. Canvasback, redheads and pintails—in that order—are what I call real ducks.

It was getting on about noon. We had already eaten our sandwiches when Ken came and said he was going to move us to another blind where he thought we would have a chance at pintails or brant. Remember, the weather had not let up a bit. Once again, I was thankful for the modern clothes.

We loaded up in the Carolina skiff for another long ride. I didn't know where we were. I did have a compass, and Brent wanted me to get it out so we could see which way the wind was blowing. I could just see the spoil area on the Ocracoke side of Hatteras Inlet. Everywhere else you looked all you could see was water. When we got to the next site, we had to walk at least one hundred yards to get to the blind. Ken said we were about one hour too late because the tide was gone around the blind except for two little potholes where the decoys were. This time the decoys were all pintail and brant.

Now we had clouds of pintail like the redheads at the other blind. Most of them would come by just out of range. I forgot to tell you, but all these boys except me are what I call good shots. We were all shooting 2¾-inch shells. My old Model 11 Remington won't take anything longer. The ducks were coming in the range of a 10-gauge or 12-gauge with 3½-inch shells. At any rate, the boys soon got four pintails, which was our limit. We didn't see a brant. It was then after 3:00 p.m., and the weather wasn't getting any better. Ken was nowhere to be seen. Nobody said much, but we were all thinking the same thing: we knew if Ken didn't soon get there, we would be spending the night in that blind because you can't see the shoals in the dark.

I said I thought we had better start conserving the water and nabs. All agreed. I started looking through my bag. I thought I had a VHF radio in there, but realized I had left it in my truck. I did find three flares, a box of dry matches and a cell phone. Brent said he had a flashlight. It was now 3:20 and there was no sign of Ken. We all knew it was getting serious.

I had one ace in my mind that I hadn't told the boys about until then. For you to fully understand this ace, I have to take you back forty-nine years to when I was in the Coast Guard. I was stationed with a friend named Herbert Lange from Brandywine, Maryland. He and his wife, Iva, have been close friends of mine ever since. Lange is now a retired chief engineman and lives near Elizabeth City. Their son Paul is a helicopter pilot stationed in Elizabeth City and is about to retire. Paul is an ace helicopter pilot. A few years ago he got a Congressional Medal for a daring rescue of nine people on a sailboat in a storm so far out in the Atlantic that he had to land on an aircraft carrier to take on fuel to get back in. The captain of the carrier commended him for being able to even land on the carrier, because the seas were so rough.

My plan was that if the cell phone would work, I was going to call Lange and ask him to get in touch with Paul, call Oden's Dock to find out where Ken's blinds were and tell him I had three flares. I think Paul would find a way to get a helicopter to come look for "Uncle Travis," as he used to call me.

Now back to the story. Just about 3:30, somebody said, "Here comes Ken." He was a welcome sight. The tide was even lower now. We could see the next blind, but we didn't know the men in it were the other sportsmen who had been with us that morning. When we picked them up, they had a nice bag of ducks. I don't remember all they had. As a matter of fact, I didn't vacate my seat in the stern to pay too much attention.

It was getting dark when we got to Oden's Dock, and I was glad to be there. In fifty-nine years of duck hunting in Currituck Sound, I guess I've been fortunate not to have had to spend the night out there. I did come close one time. I have always tried to take precautions just in case, like food, water, flares, dry matches and, now, a radio, unless I forget it.

We went back to the motel and did a repeat of Monday night: a good meal at Soundside Restaurant and back to bed. Tuesday morning, another breakfast and sandwiches to go.

When Ken put us in the blind Tuesday morning, we told him to check with us about noon. We only wanted to stay a half day, as we all had a long drive home. The wind was still blowing hard, but not as hard as Monday. The sky was crystal clear. Ken took us to the blind the other sportsmen were in Monday, and they went to the one we were in Monday afternoon. There wasn't much happening Tuesday. Plenty of ducks, but they just wouldn't come close enough. I think the sun glistening on a bright day has something to do with it. Roger got a brant and somebody got a pintail.

Brent is a good shot, but it bothers him if he misses. He reminds me in that way of an old friend who used to hunt with me, Gordon Sawyer, who was one of the "Roving Hunters" I wrote about in my first book. He was an excellent shot, but if he missed it just worried him to death. Brent had just missed when we saw Ken coming for us. Brent said, "I sure do hate to leave on a shot like that."

We got back to Oden's Dock, said our goodbyes to Ken, went to the motel to change clothes and went to Sandy's house to see what was happening

Street side of Sandy and Brenda Thorpe's "Fish House." *Author's collection.*

there. Things were happening: carpenters, painters, electricians, plumbers. It was going full blast. I think things had been happening too slowly, and Sandy was getting it in gear.

It was time for us to go our separate ways. And so ended a great time of fellowship and duck hunting…in that order.

A Fishing Trip with the McCotter Clan Is Something to Behold

First I must introduce you to Taylor Mangum. I would guess Taylor to be in his early forties. I suppose you would call him a retired young tobacco farmer. He is from Roxboro, North Carolina.

How Taylor got to Morehead City and mixed up with DeWitt McCotter, I don't know. What I do know is that Taylor and DeWitt are the best of friends, and Taylor loves to fish as much as DeWitt does. I don't know what kind of arrangement they have, but Taylor keeps the boat cleaner than it was when it came from the factory. I know they have a commercial fishing license, and they sell the fish they catch.

I first met Taylor last year when I went to Morehead to fish with McCotter. When we got to the boat that morning, Taylor had the Caterpillar engines cranked up. It sounded like two motor graders idling. The running lights were all on, the spreader lights had the cockpit lit up and, as soon as we stepped aboard, McCotter manned the helm and Taylor let the lines loose. When we got in that evening, as soon as the lines were secured, McCotter jumped on the dock, motioned for me to come on, said goodbye to Taylor and we were gone.

Now, for a poor country boy like me who has owned a boat of some kind since I was six years old, that was unbelievable service. I told McCotter he had better keep all that service quiet—I see people coming through Coinjock with million-dollar yachts who don't get that kind of "waiting on." If they could get up with Taylor, it would be bad news for McCotter.

Now that you have met Taylor Mangum, I will get on with the fishing trip. This story takes place during the October duck hunting season of 1989. On the evening of October 11, DeWitt and Fred Dunston arrived at Piney Island just in time to enjoy a drink on the front porch of the clubhouse and watch the sun set over Coinjock Bay. The mallards were flying back and forth looking for their evening meal, and the yachts were making a steady parade south on their annual migration. Just before dinner, Sandy Thorpe arrived with Clint McCotter.

Discussion at dinner was on whether they were going hunting from the club or fishing in the Gulf Stream the next morning. Of course, there was much discussion about the weather. McCotter had the VHF tuned in to the weather channel and had already heard the same report of fifteen- to twenty-five-mile-per-hour southeast winds a half dozen times.

After dinner, McCotter started pacing the floor. "Well, what are we going to do, boys?"

Of course, Clint wanted to go to the stream. He had gotten to be a real big game fisherman. This is good for McCotter because if son wants to do it, Mama thinks its fine.

"I've got to call Taylor," McCotter said. Now, you understand, McCotter couldn't take that boat to Pirate's Cove Marina in Manteo without taking Taylor along to look after it, so he rented Fred's condo at the Yachtsman for Taylor. McCotter is like the Shah of Iran; when he travels, he has to have his whole entourage. He talked to Taylor and got the word on what all the party boats had done that day, told Taylor he would call him back in a few minutes and paced some more! Much more discussion took place about whether the wind was going to blow too strong or not. Finally, the decision was made. He called Taylor and said they would be at Pirate's Cove at 5:30 a.m. They told June not to fix supper Thursday night because Clint would grill tuna.

By now, it was time for them to go to bed if they were going to be up that early. Bear in mind, this was October 12, opening day of the duck season, and nobody was hunting at Piney Island Club. Instead, they were all fishing in the Gulf Stream. I didn't know what the club was coming to!

I got back over to the club about 5:30 the next afternoon, after a hard day's work at the office. I saw Fred's Suburban there, so I knew the fishermen were back. I also saw Jimmy's boat gone, so I figured they had gone hunting. June confirmed my thoughts. She said Clint had called her from Pirates Cove about 4:00 and said they didn't catch any fish and would she please fix dinner. She was cooking deer, mashed potatoes, gravy, biscuits and peas. Need I say more?!?

I decided to get in the *Mother Goose* and ride around to Cedar Island Bay and see what was going on. I was just chugging along right slow when here came Fred and Sandy speeding up to me. They said they had their limit and wanted to get in with me. I said, "Fine," tied their boat onto the stern of *Mother Goose* and helped old fat Jewel, Jimmie's dog, in. She went straight to the cabin and lay down. She's no dumb dog.

About this time, I looked up and saw a nice little bunch of about six teal go right into Clint and DeWitt in Little Oyster Cove. It sounded like the Normandy invasion, but I only saw one little teal fall. Sam immediately hit the water to retrieve the duck. I told Fred and Sandy I thought we had just as well ease on back and watch the sunset. They agreed.

We were sitting back on the front porch enjoying a little toddy when the other two came in with their one teal. When McCotter got up there to join us, he said he had been from four thousand feet of water in the Gulf Stream to six inches of water in Oyster Cove in one day.

They were all tired, so it was decided that they would not fish on Friday, but would hunt. Of course, this took several calls back and forth to Taylor, but the decision was finally made.

After breakfast Friday morning, we decided to take the *Frances M*, my boat, on a leisurely cruise up to Pungo, Virginia. The waterway was full of yachts going south and this would make a change of pace from the fast sportfisherman. The old boat was slow, but you could ride and snooze in air-conditioned comfort. I did catch a few of them sacked out making zzz's. They seemed to enjoy the trip.

As soon as we hit the dock when we got back, McCotter was running for the car so he could catch the evening fly. I told them to go ahead, that I would see them at dinner. Since I don't have Taylor, I had to do the chores on my boat that Taylor does for McCotter.

After dinner, Sandy left to help move his daughter to Raleigh on Saturday. I was scheduled to fish with the others on Saturday. Fred couldn't decide whether to fish with McCotter or Earl Goodwin on Saturday. Earl was going to fish for Spanish mackerel closer to shore and Fred wanted to catch fish. The boats had been catching a lot of them. Fred knew that if he went with McCotter, it was full throttle to the Gulf Stream, big fish or none! Of course, we had to call Taylor to find out what was going on. Taylor must have had a lot of news, since this turned out to be a long call. Fred was still in a dilemma. He couldn't decide what to do. DeWitt told Taylor he didn't know what Fred was going to do, but that he, Clint, Jimmy and I would be there at 5:30 in the morning. Fred finally decided to go with Earl.

I had decided to spend the night at the club on Frances's recommendation. She could do without being awakened at four o'clock on a Saturday! I gathered up some potted meat, crackers, Vienna sausage and Cokes before I left home. I learned from the fishing trip in Morehead that if you want anything to eat when you are with McCotter you damn well better get it yourself. He claims to just eat ice all day. However, when lunchtime came Saturday, I saw some hands pass up a sandwich to him on the bridge. I never did figure if it was Taylor or Clint.

Howard Cliborne went up to hunt on Friday afternoon. It seems that since McCotter had discovered the fishing out of Oregon Inlet, his wife, Denny, had contacted Howard about renting a place from him down there for two months the next summer. Remember what I told you about McCotter and his entourage.

The *Frances M. Author's collection.*

We drove three vehicles to Pirates Cove Saturday morning. Fred was not going back to Piney Island. DeWitt and Clint were going to stay with Taylor because Howard wanted to show them some places to rent the next summer (frankly, my prediction was that McCotter would own a place in Nags Head before then). I was going to drive too, because Jimmy and I had to get back to Piney Island.

Four o'clock came early. Jimmy had the coffee and sweet rolls ready, and we were off to Pirates Cove. McCotter, now turning into Captain McCotter, ordered me to stop by the 7-11 and get him a bag of ice to eat. Aye, aye, sir!

We arrived at Pirates Cove on time. Taylor had the boat ready for sea and was chomping at the bit to go. I jumped on, scared I was going to get left. But I soon noticed we didn't go anywhere. Captain McCotter was pacing back and forth in the cockpit and looking up the dock. The Caterpillars were roaring. In fact, I had to stand up on the bridge in order to get a breath of fresh air. The smoke was about to get me. It finally dawned on me that our captain was waiting for one of the local boys to lead him down that narrow, dark channel in Roanoke Sound. All of a sudden, Captain McCotter sprang to the bridge, pushed the levers ahead on the Cats and we were off. The bridge opened, and after the whole fleet had passed through, everybody's throttles were pushed forward. The whole fleet was moving down this narrow channel at between twenty-five and thirty miles per hour.

The *Pelican* going out Hatteras Inlet at twenty-eight knots. *Author's collection.*

I braced myself the best I could because I knew if that boat ahead of us stopped or ran aground we would be in his cockpit. Our captain had his hand upon the throttle and his eye upon that mast light ahead of him. Nobody uttered a word.

When we got down to the intersection of Old House Channel, we intercepted the Oregon Inlet Fishing Center Fleet. Now we had a string of boats almost as far as you could see in both directions. It was just a string of running lights traveling at a very high speed. A very impressive sight.

As the boats went under the Bonner Bridge heading out to sea, Omie Tillet said a prayer, which was really a mini-sermon, over the VHF radio asking for the safe return of the fleet. I'm told he does this every day and nobody interrupts him. Omie is a legend on the Outer Banks as a boatbuilder, charter boat captain and founder of Sam and Omie's restaurant.

When we reached the sea buoy, our captain punched in the loran numbers to take us thirty-eight nautical miles offshore where the water is four thousand feet deep and blue as indigo, and the tuna are supposed to be swimming. The autopilot took over. The captain punched another button on the Loran and said we would be there in one hour and so many minutes. He just sat back like Garfield and let those "Cats" purr. I decided it was time for me to go down and have a few Fig Newtons.

A Fishing Trip with the McCotter Clan Is Something to Behold

Left to right: Clint McCotter, Taylor Mangum and Jimmy Markert. *Author's collection.*

We were fishing shortly after 8:00 a.m. The temperature of the Gulf Stream was eighty-one degrees, with a light chop. The sea was working alive with porpoise. Sometimes two at a time would jump clear out of the water.

It was not long before a reel started singing. Clint grabbed the harness, and the captain was fussing because it took him so long to get it on. The captain and Taylor decided it was a wahoo. Soon Clint had the fight out of the fish, and he was boated. The experts estimated him to be thirty-five pounds. It was not long before another reel was singing. Now it was Jimmy's turn. It was another wahoo. He was fighting so hard that Jimmy started tightening the drag on the reel. Taylor hollered and told Captain McCotter that Jimmy was messing with the drag. That is a no-no on that boat, the captain said. "Taylor sets the drag and nobody messes with it." I thought we were going to have mutiny. The fish was finally boated and estimated to be forty-five pounds.

We trolled for a good while. There were lots of other boats out there doing the same thing. Then, there was a big hit. The fish went deep. The captain gave the order to take in all the other reels. Clint had on the fighting harness, but the fish was still going. The captain started backing down to help him and said there must have been five hundred yards of line out. Then Clint started making progress, but soon there was no more fight. It was like reeling in a log. Somebody suggested the line was wrapped in his tail. When he got in close enough to see, we realized there was no tail at all. A shark had bit him in half. The experts (no need to name them) estimated him to have been a fifty-pound tuna.

There were no more strikes, just fishing. While riding around out there, I had plenty of time to think. I couldn't help but think of all the men who lost their lives right in those same waters in 1942. Most of you who will read this don't know how close World War II was to the United States. Most of you were not born, but the ones who are old enough to remember the war knew nothing of the ship sinkings because the War Department didn't want it publicized just how successful the Germans were. I remember one night seeing three tankers burn off Nags Head. Mama, Daddy and I were staying at the old First Colony Inn at the time. Also, at home, I lay in my bed nights during that year and heard explosions at sea. The way the crow flies, the sea is only eight miles from where I was raised at Coinjock. One night I thought it was going to break the windows in the house. The next day we heard that the Germans had torpedoed an ammunition ship off Corolla. When I looked at that tuna, I couldn't help thinking how easily a shark could bite a man in two.

The captain said at 2:00 p.m. to take the reels in and we'd head home. Since that tuna got cut in two and could not be sold, Captain McCotter had been mulling in his mind about how it would taste. He asked me if he came back to Piney Island would I come eat supper with him. I assured him I would. He checked with Clint, since he is the chief tuna chef. That was fine with Clint.

Taylor reminded the captain to stop by the icehouse in Wanchese and get ice for the next day. They could get ice there for nothing.

When we got to the icehouse, there was only a short space at the dock. McCotter had his doubts about trying to get in there. I assured him there was plenty of room and he put her right in the spot, whereupon I told him I couldn't have done better myself, but I could have done as well!

When we got back to the dock, somehow Taylor got talked into cleaning that tuna for us. Jimmy and I stopped by Food Lion and got salad makings and potatoes to bake. We got back to Piney Island, and Clint did a magnificent job of grilling the tuna.

Maybe you wonder why I was not on the business end of one of those reels. At the beginning of this journey, I told the captain and Taylor that I had roped enough calves when I was young and I had no desire to rope one of those big fish. I preferred to watch them do it. If all the lines got full and it became necessary, I would do my part, but only out of necessity.

Now you know what a fishing trip with the McCotter clan is like.

A World-class Fishing Trip on the *Pelican*

Sandy Thorpe had told me during the duck hunting season that he was going to have the *Pelican*, his forty-six-foot Buddy Smith sportfisherman, at the Hatteras Marlin Club in February of 1996. He was going to try to catch some of those bigeye tuna.

It turned out he went down a little earlier and he called me on January 29. He said they'd had a good day fishing and for me to be at the boat at 6:00 a.m. We would go to Sunny's Restaurant for breakfast. He told me to call Jimmy Markert and tell Jimmy to see if Frankie Helms wanted to go. I called Jimmy, and he said he'd call Frankie and get right back to me. He called me right back and all was set to go. I was to meet Jimmy at Henry's Texaco in Coinjock at 4:00 a.m., and we were to pick up Frankie at Jarvisburg Junction shortly thereafter.

I called Sandy and told him we'd be there. McCotter fished Monday and decided to stay over and fish with me Tuesday. Sandy said McCotter wanted to talk to me. McCotter told me to bring food. He said Sandy didn't have anything to eat on the boat. He said he got so hungry he thought he was going to have to eat the bait. I assured him food would be no problem. I told him Jo Ann was making ham sandwiches right then. She made ten ham sandwiches, packed a box of honey buns, a box of oatmeal pies, nabs, apples, canned tuna salad, canned chicken salad, Vienna sausage, Deviled ham, crackers and Hostess apple and cherry pies.

My alarm went off at 3:15 a.m. I got ready and we had decided I would drive Jo Ann's pickup truck instead of my Jeep since the Jeep had some mechanical problems. Her truck has a back seat. Jimmy and Frankie are big men, so I chose to stretch out on the back seat and let Jimmy drive. Jimmy arrived at Henry's at exactly 4:00 a.m. We went on and picked up Frankie. We arrived in Hatteras at 6:30. We all piled in Jim's (Sandy's Captain's) Suburban and headed for Sunny's, where we met DeWitt McCotter and Brent Nash. They had stayed in a motel. I had met Brent many years earlier, so we were not strangers. Then Sandy's mate, Pico, joined us for breakfast.

Travis Morris and DeWitt McCotter enjoying oysters at the "Fish House" *Author's collection.*

After a hearty breakfast, we went back to the boat and Jim got those big Mann engines cranked up and we headed for sea. Now let me tell you here and now that today was the first time I have ever been in the ocean with McCotter when he was not captain. I will give him credit. He behaved very well.

McCotter did exert one little bit of authority that nobody knows about until now. I thought we were going to the Gulf Stream and I dressed for that, but I found out these fish are not in the Gulf Stream. When I got in the boat that morning, it was cold in there. I asked McCotter whether that boat had any heat. He said it did, but Sandy wouldn't turn it on. McCotter said he like to froze to death the day before. About this time, Sandy came out of his stateroom dressed like an Eskimo. He could have gone to the North Pole. When I saw that I said to myself, "Old boy, your ass is in for a freezing today!" Thanks to McCotter, that didn't happen. When we were heading out the inlet, nobody was in the cabin but McCotter and me.

"There is one advantage to being a captain," McCotter said, "you know where everything is." With that, he changed the heat from sixty-one to sixty-nine degrees and that made for a pleasant day.

We soon reached the fishing ground and it was decided that Jimmy Markert would get in the chair first. This is a new kind of fishing to me. First, the cranker was tied in the fighting chair with ropes. I guess this is so the fish can't pull him overboard. The cranker had a big rod and a monster reel. Pico had a five-gallon bucket of shad that he had chopped up. He started throwing these pieces overboard to chum the fish. There were boats all around us doing the same thing. For a few minutes, nothing happened. Then one hit the bait and, man, did he hit it! He had that monster reel screaming and, before the line was all out, he broke it and was gone. "The one that got away." We will always wonder how big he was. It took Jimmy at least five minutes to reel in the slack.

By then there was a fish hitting every piece of chum that was thrown out. These fish were not minnows. They were from two to five hundred pounds! Nobody had ever seen anything like that. Pico rigged another hook and, as soon as the bait hit the water, a big fish hit it. Jimmy Markert is a strong, robust man, but the fish was about to get the best of him. Now if you think Jimmy is big, Frankie is real big. And I don't mean fat. He is a commercial fisherman with hard muscles. Now, Frankie saw the fish about to get the best of his friend and everybody was teasing Jimmy about the fish wearing him out, so Frankie grabbed hold of the rod with Jimmy and started helping him pull back on the rod. After a fight that lasted at least thirty minutes, they finally got the fish up to the side of the boat where he could be tagged and released. I heard estimations of the weight of this fish that were from three to five hundred pounds. He was a big fish that took the fight out of Jimmy.

Jimmy Markert in the chair with Frankie Helms helping him bring in a bigeye tuna. *Author's collection.*

By then the ocean was alive with bigeye tuna. Nobody on board had ever seen anything like it. All the charter and private boats were gathered over an area of ten to fifteen acres and everybody was chumming and catching fish. Jimmy said one time that he saw ten or twelve fish running like bullets for the chum. I have heard that people come from all over the world to charter boats to catch these fish at Hatteras. I felt very privileged to be a part of it.

I believe the next man in the chair was Brent Nash. As soon as the bait hit the water, the fish hit it. Most of these fish were running 200 to 250 pounds. The law will allow you to bring in one fish per boat per day provided the fish is not over seventy-three inches long. Everybody had a turn in the chair, including Captain McCotter. This was a sight I had never seen before. I have never seen him do anything but run his own boat. He doesn't touch a line, bait or a scrub brush. He just runs the boat and gives orders.

After McCotter landed his fish, Captain Jim got in the chair and landed a couple. Nobody had a problem getting the fish to the boat except Jimmy. Since Jimmy is a strong young man, I have to believe his fish was much bigger than the others. Sandy wanted me to get in the chair, but I didn't have to think twice about that. It might just be my luck to hang one of those bad boys that was as big or bigger than Jimmy's, and once you are in that chair tied down and have a fish on, you can't get out and turn it over to someone else.

I don't have anything to prove to those fish, but I am an old man with a young wife. I wasn't about to take a chance on getting myself out of whack. Jimmy was still worn out when he was driving us home.

One thing I did try and enjoy was a spinning reel Sandy had with what he called a "popper" on it with no hooks. It was a plug about six inches long. I would cast that and every time it hit the water a fish would grab it and go with it for a ways. Then he would realize it wasn't real and would turn it loose.

Brent wanted to try to hook one on his fly rod, which he did, but he didn't land any, of course. They took one fish aboard that was just under the legal keeping size. Pico had to cut his head off to get him in the fish box.

It was about 12:30 in the afternoon, and we had caught twelve or thirteen bigeye tuna. All hands had worked the fight out of themselves and they decided it was time to go ashore. We got back to the Marlin Club, and as soon as we got the lines on the fuel dock, McCotter took off for the motel to get a shower so he could head for Rocky Mount.

After we fueled and got backed into the slip, Frankie carved up the tuna into steaks while the rest of us watched, except Pico. He was washing down the *Pelican.*

McCotter came back all slicked down and got some zip-lock bags of tuna and said he was going to stop at the Red & White and get a cooler. I decided I had better get one, too. When I got to the store, McCotter was coming out and said they didn't have any coolers. He had bought a package of garbage bags and put his tuna in one of them with twenty pounds of ice. He gave me the rest of the box, and I bought ice and did the same. I wonder what the back of that Lexus smelled like when he got back to Rocky Mount and that ice had melted out of that bag!

We all said our goodbyes and thanked Sandy for a wonderful day of world-class fishing. I don't know how it could be topped.

When I got home, I called McCotter just to rehash our good day. Denny said he should be home in thirty minutes. I told Jo Ann that McCotter had stopped at Sunnyside Oyster Bar in Williamston because he had had time to get home.

Let me say in closing that I feel very fortunate to have friends like Sandy Thorpe, DeWitt McCotter and Lindy Dunn, not just because they are kind enough to share with me good times on their beautiful boats, but because I know they are my true friends in foul weather as well as fair. The sun is setting for me, and I hope it's time for a little fair weather.

Left to right: Mort Neblett, Sandy Thorpe and DeWitt McCotter eating at Sandy's "Fish House." *Author's collection.*

Left to right: Brenda Thorpe, Travis Morris and Jo Ann Morris. I always enjoy the company of good-looking women! *Author's collection.*

When we go fishing, I don't fish. I just go along to record what happened and enjoy the company of my friends. To quote a plaque Sandy recently gave me, "Believe me, my young friend, there is nothing, absolutely nothing, half so much worth doing as simply messing around in boats."

Thanks again, Sandy, for a day of world-class fishing on the *Pelican*.

Rock Fishing in Coinjock

The early duck season started October 3, 2001. I quit hunting in this warm, early season several years ago when DeWitt McCotter and I almost stepped on a cottonmouth in a blind; that blind is now called the "Snake Blind."

Wash Bishop and Mike Feasel hadn't yet had that experience and were down there hunting. Wash got that experience before he left by almost putting his hand on a cottonmouth that was coiled up under the cover on his motor.

Fred Dunstan got to the club at Piney Island late Thursday afternoon and said he thought he'd pass up the duck hunting for rock fishing. I told him I believed I'd go with him. The season didn't come in until October 17, but you can catch them and throw them back.

Fred told me to be at the club at seven o'clock the next morning. I got there with a couple of Hobo sandwiches from Kevin's Amoco and a couple of rounds of coffee. After eating, we put the boat over. She spun like a sewing machine, but wouldn't hit a lick. He messed with the choke. Still nothing.

"I'll go home and get my boat," I told him. When I got home, the battery on my Maycraft was as dead as a doornail, but when I hit the starter on the old Polar Craft I'd gotten from Sandy Thorpe, she rolled right over. I hooked her up to my old Jeep and off I went. I did notice, however, that my trailer license had expired in February, but said to myself, "I don't have time to worry about that. We got to go fishing!"

I was soon at Piney Island and backed the Polar Craft overboard and hit the starter. As soon as she rolled over, the old Johnson started right up. We got our gear in the boat and then I stuffed my ears with cotton and pulled a hood up over my head so as to keep from getting a headache. I pushed the throttle down and we were off for Coinjock. We were idling along in front of the marinas and stopped at the old Coast Guard station and made a few casts where I had caught rock before. No luck, so we decided to go down to the bridge. When we got about along where the old bridge had been, I saw

Bill Williams and another man standing on the bank fishing. Bill was pulling in a big rock. We knew the fish were in the canal.

We went on down to the new bridge and it seemed every time Fred would cast he would hang it in a bridge fender or a piling. We decided to go back to where we had seen Bill catch that rock. When we got there, both men were pulling in rock. Fred hollered and asked them what kind of bait they were using. They had a rig with two green bucktails. We didn't have anything like that, but we had something green. Bill said there was a hole right in front of where he was. He said to cast from the side of the canal and pull it back toward the bank. We caught three or four, but were not catching them like those fellows were. We decided we'd go back to Piney Island and go to Currituck Sports and get some baits like those fellows were using. We fired up the Johnson and off we went.

When we got to Piney Island, Wash was getting ready to go home. Fred and I went to Currituck Sports. I bought eight baits and Fred bought ten or twelve. We got back to the club and made a sandwich. Mike said he didn't have time to go with us in the boat, so he would fish from the bank. Fred gave him two or three lures and we took off. When we got to Coinjock, Bill was gone, so we tied up where he had been. On my first cast I caught two.

I called Jo Ann on my cell phone and told her what we were doing. I know she loves to catch fish, so I told her to meet us at the end of the old Coinjock road and get in the boat with us. Then she could go back to the store when she wanted to. She wouldn't do it. She said she didn't have an hour to take off from the store. She doesn't have the same philosophy I have about the business. Her business comes ahead of everything. I guess that is why she has something and I have nothing, but I don't plan to change at this late date in my life.

We didn't catch anything under about twenty-two inches. When you catch two fish at a time that size on a little rod and reel, you have a fight on your hands. At least three times I caught two at a time. I don't know how many times Fred caught two at a time. The problem was there were hangs on the bottom and we were losing our lures fast. We figured if we went across the canal to the south side maybe we wouldn't get hung so bad. We tied up over there and we were still catching the rock, but were still getting hung. Just about the time we lost our last lure, Mike drove up and started fishing from the bank. We had landed twenty-one, not counting the ones we lost on hangs.

Fred had to take his boat to Camden to get it worked on, so we called the fishing quits. We got back to Piney Island and put the boat on the trailer and I carried it home. I was on edge that a cop would see my expired trailer tags, but I was lucky.

Travis Morris with his catch of the day from the canal, a nice rock. *Author's collection.*

Fred Dunstan with a rockfish from the Coinjock Canal. *Author's collection.*

After I got the boat home, I went back to Currituck Sports to get some lures in case Jo Ann wanted to go fishing when she got off work. The first person I saw when I got there was Mike Feasel. I asked him if he'd caught any fish and he said, "Oh yes! That's why I'm in here buying lures for the next time I come." It was going on toward 4:00 p.m. and I decided a nap was more in order than going back to the office. And so ended the best day of rock fishing I ever had.

Something to remember is that when the ducks or fish are having a meeting and you want to participate, you had better cancel your meetings and go because they are not going to cancel theirs to wait for you!

Trucks and Truck Farming

The hunting and fishing stories I have told were just one part of life in Currituck County during the early years. For many of us in Currituck, the background was filled in with farming and truck farming. For most people, there was no such thing as doing one job and being able to make it through the year. You had to work with the seasons, which meant some people farmed, fished and hunted in order to make ends meet. I wound up truck farming for many years and doing some guiding in the winter months. This book would not present a clear picture of how it was to make a living in Currituck without including this section on truck farming in what would now be called the "old days." It was only after getting into the real estate business in the seventies that my life got more relaxed and I was able to enjoy the "modern" fishing and hunting trips that I have told of.

When I was growing up, lower Currituck County was strictly a truck farming area; by that I mean vegetables. The main crops were Irish potatoes, cabbage, snap beans, sweet potatoes, tomatoes, watermelon, cauliflower and some bell peppers.

Trucks would get loaded here one afternoon and catch the Chesapeake Bay Ferry that night from Little Creek, Virginia, to Cape Charles. Then they would work their way on up the shore until they got to George Trivett's place in Newcastle, Delaware: the Black Cat. The local shippers knew all the trucks would stop there, so if they had any further instructions for the drivers, they would call the Black Cat. That night they would go on to New York Market. The Washington Street Market was where the World Trade Center stood until 2001. It was built in the 1800s for horse and wagons. Nothing over thirty-three feet could park there. Everything else had to park out under what we called the Vie Dock or Westside elevated highway. The reason ten-wheelers were so popular was they could go right on Washington Street. It cost the shippers a dime to get produce hauled from the Vie Dock to Washington Street.

The trucks in those days were just plain two-ton Fords, Chevrolets and Dodges pulling single-axle and tandem-axle trailers. I remember when a thirty-two-foot trailer was really a long trailer. A 22 White or a K10 International was really a big truck. These were gas jobs also; diesels hadn't been heard of around here then.

There was another market called the Bronx Terminal Market. It was right next to Yankee Stadium. When they renovated downtown Manhattan and built the World Trade Center, they moved the Washington Street Market to Hunt's Point in the Bronx.

When I was a kid sitting out under the old oaks watching those trucks go by at night, there was just something intriguing about them, wondering where they were going. I loved to hear those old Fords and Chevrolets moaning. I wished I were driving one of them, but time would take care of that.

Trucking was so different in the fifties and sixties when I was doing it. There were not modern truck stops like you find all up and down the interstate today. In fact, there were no interstates.

The only interstate highway between Currituck and Florida when I started trucking was from Kenly to Fayetteville, North Carolina. Most all the other roads I rode to Belle Glade, Florida, were two lanes.

We had to eat wherever we could find a place that had room to pull the truck off the road. A lot of times, this was a country grocery store or service station. Service stations were the main places we could find a restroom. I always kept a bucket in the ice bunker or under the sleeper (if the truck had one) for emergencies.

Showers were hard to find. There was one at Eagles Nest Truck Stop in Savannah, Georgia, and one at Across the Border Truck Stop in St. Augustine, Florida. We couldn't afford motel rooms very often, although they were only about five or seven dollars.

We always carried spare tires, even when they were as slick as the palm of your hand; they'd run in cold weather. We didn't call anybody to change our tires; we changed them ourselves. These are not just experiences I had, but represent what most of the truckers hauling produce experienced in the fifties and sixties.

The first truckers I knew of around here were Mr. Walton Meiggs (Frances's daddy); Mr. Will Doxey; two of his sons, Melvin and Ikey; Mr. Doxey's son-in-law, Willard Lane; and Mr. Will Edwards, whose daughter married Melvin Doxey. Mr. Will Edwards used to run a freight boat to Norfolk before they had trucks, so I've been told. Mr. Grady Griggs (of Griggs Lumber and Produce) had several trucks. Lee Smith had three, Harold Woodhouse had three, Ambrose Dozier had two, Bernard Evans Jr. had one, Wilson Corbel and Barlow Beasley had one. There were so many people in Currituck County who owned or drove trucks, I cannot begin to name them all. These are just a few of the people I can remember having trucks at one time or another in Currituck, so you can see there was a lot of produce raised here. Mr. Meiggs, Mr. Doxey and Mr. Edwards started in the thirties; the others were from the forties through the sixties.

I started farming in 1955 and bought my first ten-wheeler in 1956. It was a 1948 Ford that I bought from Mr. Will Doxey. Back then the seed potatoes would come on a ship from Prince Edward Island, Canada, to Lambert's Point Pier in Norfolk, Virginia. We would start in January hauling these potatoes from Norfolk to the local packinghouses. Then we would haul fertilizer from the Royster, Smith Douglas or Weaver Fertilizer plants in Norfolk. By the time the fertilizer hauling was over, it was time to start hauling spring cabbage, then snap beans, then potatoes. There would be a little slack spell between potatoes and watermelons. Then we would start hauling corn to Norfolk and up the eastern shore to the chicken houses. In October, there would be fall snap beans and cabbage; in November and December, soybeans.

My first long-distance trip was in the fall of 1956. Don Alexander was managing Currituck Exchange for Smith Douglas Company and asked me if I would take a load of cabbage to Baltimore for him. He couldn't get a truck. I told him I would, so we loaded up the old ten-wheeler. I got my toolbox, a pillow and blanket and headed up the road. I had never been to Baltimore. I remember that afternoon as if it were yesterday. I was heading up 460 from Suffolk to Petersburg. It was a beautiful fall day. Farmers were picking peanuts in the fields and country stores had piles of pumpkins out front.

By the time I got to Petersburg, the hills were getting so steep I was afraid the old Ford might not make it. This was before the days of the Richmond-Petersburg Turnpike, or I-95. It was 301 or U.S. 1. I stopped at an icehouse at the top of a hill between Richmond and Petersburg. I had to blow ice on the cabbage, then I asked the attendant how much worse the hills got between there and Baltimore and also which road was flatter. He said the hills got longer and not as steep, and 301 was a little flatter. The next thing that happened was my first introduction to dishonesty on the road. When I got ready to pay my bill for the ice, the attendant wanted to know how much I wanted a ticket for. I'm sure I looked startled, and said, "Just for the amount I got." He said, "Everybody else pads the tickets." I said, "Well, not me." You see, the shippers pay for the ice.

I got the old Ford underway again and when I got to 301 there was a sign as big as the side of a house that said, "No trucks with over two axles for the next 23 miles." Believe it or not, I didn't see it and headed her right on north on 301! When I got about a mile from where big trucks could ride 301, a patrolman stopped me. I thought to myself, "What have I done now?" Then he proceeded to tell me. Somehow I managed to talk him out of giving me a ticket. I got going again and, when I got in sight of the Potomac River Bridge, cars looked like matchboxes up there. I said, "Lord, this old Ford ain't going to make that," but she did.

I finally found my way to the commission house on Light Street in Baltimore. I parked the truck and cut her off. Presney (Currituck-ese for "after a while"), I started to get cold and was going to start her up and get warm. When I hit the starter, she wouldn't turn over, but it wasn't like a dead battery. I got out and checked the oil and it was milky and to the top of the dipstick. My heart liked to have jumped out. I knew I was in trouble. I walked down the street to a service station and got a big empty can and some new oil. I went back and drained the oil and filled up with the new. She started right up. I let it run a few minutes, then cut it off and checked the oil; the same thing. I made another trip to the service station and drained the oil again. I also got water from somewhere to fill the radiator up. About this time the commission merchant came down and opened up. He told me he wanted me to carry the cabbage to an A&P somewhere. I told him my situation and said I couldn't carry them anywhere, so he unloaded me there. He told me where there was an all-night service station a few blocks away. When I got there, the attendant said he didn't have a mechanic at night, but I could work on it myself. The first thing I did was pull the spark plugs out one at a time and crank her over to see which cylinder the water was going in. I soon found it and pulled that head. I was in luck. I saw that it was a blown head gasket. The service station man told me where there was an all-night parts place, so I got a cab there. As luck would have it, the only one he had was for the side I didn't need. I went back and had to wait until the Ford place opened the next morning. It was in walking distance. I put the gasket on and headed for Currituck. I only had about thirty dollars in my pocket. I figured if I could get to Brandywine, I could leave the truck at my friend Lange's daddy's house and catch the bus home, but she took me right on to Currituck.

Daddy had given me a herd of cattle that he had for a hobby when I started farming. It seemed to me every time Frances and I started to go somewhere, Mama would call and say a calf was out. I had already knocked my front tooth out one day when it was snowing and I was nailing a board on a stable a calf was in when the nail ricocheted. I decided to turn those cows into a new Ford ten-wheeler. This was 1957. In 1959, I bought another ten-wheeler. I had two bodies for this one: an open body that would carry as many cabbages as a thirty-two-foot trailer and a refrigerated body.

I had a 1951 Ford farm truck that I had welded an extra set of wheels on to haul fertilizer and potatoes around the farm. In the spring of 1958,

I had an F800 Ford and thirty-two-foot Dorsey trailer. This was the truck Sam Waterfield was driving on the trip to Milwaukee, Wisconsin, when the transmission went out in Hammond, Indiana. *Author's collection.*

Don Alexander couldn't get trucks and talked me into loading that old Ford to go to Washington Street in New York. I had been working in the field all day when he called and I was tired, but we also needed the money. I told him if he would get it loaded for me while I ate supper and took a bath, I'd go. Late that night I pulled out. I got a couple hours of sleep going across Chesapeake Bay on the old ferry. When we docked, I headed her on up the shore. About dawn the next morning, I met Fred Simon in Delaware coming back from New York with my '57 Ford ten-wheeler. I blinked the lights and got him to stop. I offered him a good deal if he would take that old truck to New York. Fred later said when I was pulling off in the new truck that he wished we had loaded the cabbage onto that truck.

When I got home, the phone was ringing. The old Ford had thrown the blades off the fan going over the Delaware Memorial Bridge and Harold Woodhouse's truck pushed him across the top. It had a grill guard on it. He had gotten that fixed, and when he called me he was in New Jersey and said the unit wheels kept running off. By this time, Cokey (another fellow who drove for me) had come in with the Chevrolet tractor and trailer. I got him to take the ten-wheeler to New Jersey and take Fred's cabbage on to New York. I called Fred and told him what I was doing and told him to throw the unit wheels in the back of the truck and come home. Fred called me again from Salisbury, Maryland, and said the clutch was burned out. I told him I'd be there as soon as I could get there with the Chevrolet tractor and a pipe and chain. When I got that thing home, I was so disgusted with it I left it in the yard for about three months before I fixed it.

Joe Ringer and Sam Waterfield were running a garage at Coinjock and just didn't have enough business to make it. I had an old F8 Ford that I had bought to haul my own stuff around with. Sam kept after me to let him haul produce

1961 B-61 Mack that I bought new for Buck Hall to drive. My middle daughter, Wayne, is standing by the front wheel in this picture, in the front yard of our house in Currituck. I drove Mack trucks from Florida to Massachusetts. I drove them across the Appalachians, Alleghenies, Blue Ridge and Smokey Mountains, all without a "Jake Brake." I didn't mind driving in New York City, but I hated driving the mountains and didn't do it any more than I had to. *Author's collection.*

with that truck and I finally agreed. He hauled a few loads around. Then one day he loaded cabbage at Mr. Woodhouse's and, after he got loaded, he found out they were going to A&P in Milwaukee, Wisconsin. When he told me that, I called everybody I could think of to try to get them to pull my trailer for free if they would just take the load. Nobody would take it.

Sam said he thought she would make it, so he headed out. The phone rang the next night and he was in Hammond, Indiana. The transmission had gone

1956 Chevrolet truck and thirty-two-foot Trailmobile trailer. Sam Waterfield was working with me at the time. This was the truck I was driving when I saw Florida for the first time. Both of us were riding this straight cab truck. I thought when I got to the Florida line it was going to turn to warm weather and palm trees. It was not like that! My first wife, Frances, drove the truck one time to Shawboro to get her hair fixed at Aileen Holden's beauty shop. *Author's collection.*

out. He got another truck to take the cabbage on to Wisconsin and some man was kind enough to let him use his garage. Sam found a transmission in a wrecked truck that the housing was busted on, but Sam took the insides out of that and put them in my housing and brought the old Ford home.

Leamon Woodley, a black man known as "Biggy," must have driven a million miles for me. He chewed tobacco, was dirty and was rough on the truck, but he was intelligent and dependable. Remember that word "dependable." It will make up for a lot of other shortcomings.

When Biggy went out with a load, I could go to bed and go to sleep because I knew he would do everything in his power to get that load to its destination on time. If it needed to be kept cool, he would keep it cool; or, in cold weather, he would keep it from freezing. I remember one time in Boston, he bought a gas stove and put it in the ice bunker to keep a load of fruit from freezing. This was before produce trucks had Thermokings.

On the other hand, if the phone rang in the middle of the night and Biggy was on the other end, I knew I had better start putting my pants on because something bad was wrong. I remember one night he came in with an old B61 Mack with matchsticks under the springs to the generator brushes, but she was genning!

All fruit loaded in Florida had to have an inspection ticket that had to be collected at the Florida/Georgia line. Somehow Biggy got out of Florida without coming by the inspection station and, of course, his ticket was not turned in. The man who was in charge of the inspections for the state of Florida called me one day and said one of my trucks had gotten out of the

1962 B61 Mack. *Author's collection.*

state without giving up the ticket and it was very embarrassing; he wanted to know if I could please help him get that ticket. I told him I didn't know how the driver got out of Florida, but I had the ticket and would be glad to send it to him. He thanked me and gave me his home and work numbers and said if I ever had any trouble with inspections in Florida, day or night, to call him. I kept his name and number as long as I was in the business.

One time, Biggy loaded vegetables in Belle Glade, Florida, and I loaded fruit in Winter Garden. We were both going to the same man in the Bronx Terminal Market in New York. I hadn't seen him since we left Currituck going south. When I got across the Chesapeake Bay Bridge that Sunday afternoon, it started snowing. When I went by C&D Truck Stop in Pocomoke, Maryland, I saw my old Mack parked in a line of trucks. I said to myself, "Well, Biggy was ahead of me, but he is getting a few winks." I kept on driving and it seemed like it kept snowing harder. I was up on the Jersey Turnpike when I looked out the mirror and saw this truck coming up beside me; when he got up to me, the old fender was just shaking and, about that time, I saw my name on the door. Biggy was heading that old B61 for the Big Apple. The snow was flying like spray from a boat, but when I got to the market, he was already backed in.

Buck Hall and Thomas Taylor standing beside a new 1965 Peterbilt we bought from Hargrave Peterbilt in Orlando, Florida. Thomas drove a truck for Mr. Walton Meiggs (Frances's daddy) before he went in the army for World War II. When he retired out of the army, he came back to Currituck and drove with me a year or two before going into the insurance business. *Author's collection.*

I used to stay on Biggy about staying clean, so he started spraying down with cologne just before he came in the house to bring his tickets. I think he sprayed the tickets, too, because I could always tell his tickets from the other drivers' tickets by the smell.

On the first brand-new ten-wheeler I had, the cab was red and I was going to paint the body red or green like everybody else. Frances insisted I paint the body white outside, red inside, with the metal trim black. I told her I wasn't going to have my truck looking like a fish truck, but she won out and I was glad she did. I had good cabbage that year and those people on the market recognized that truck; they all wanted cabbage off that white-bodied truck. It got to the point that Benny Doff, the man I was selling to, wouldn't take them unless they came off that truck because his customers wanted them from that truck.

My son, Walton, and I drove this old Kenworth K-100 for ten years from May to September hauling produce from the market in Columbia, South Carolina, and Hammonton, New Jersey, to his roadside market in Barco, North Carolina. *Author's collection.*

It is a pleasure driving Walton's new L-900 Kenworth. It has a 525-horsepower Cummins engine with cruise control, air ride, two beds, refrigerator and TV. It's better than riding in a car. It has all the bells and whistles. I'm not used to such comfort. I have to admit I like to crack the window once in a while when we are taking off so I can listen to that turbo scream! It sounds like a jet on the tarmac. *Author's collection.*

People always recognize Walt's market from the unique signs and the antique tractors he has lined up along the roadside leading to it. *Author's collection.*

My son, Walton Morris, getting ready to go with Hambone and me to take lumber to Corolla for Kenyon Wilson's house, the first oceanfront house to be built in Corolla. *Author's collection.*

In addition to my own produce, I was buying cabbage and potatoes for Mr. Doff around here. I got freight plus ten cents a package.

It had gotten to where I had to start hauling out of Florida in order to keep drivers busy year-round. By the fall of 1963, I had three Mack trucks with payments of over $2,000 a month. That was a lot of money in 1963. The only connections I had in Florida were through a truck broker. We had a big freeze that year and it caught two of my trucks in Florida. Biggy was driving one and Buck Hall the other. Frances was in the hospital having Rhonda and I didn't know how I was going to get her out because I didn't have any money. I didn't know what to do, but I decided to call Mr. Doff. I had only hauled for him out of Currituck and didn't even know what he got out of Florida or who was hauling it. I called him and told him my situation and asked him if there was anything he could do for me. He said he didn't know, but he would see. He asked me where the trucks were and how he could get in touch with the drivers.

Three days had passed and I hadn't heard anything; I'm sure I hadn't helped boost Frances's morale in the hospital. When I got home from the hospital on the third day, I had a call from Buck Hall. He was in Belle Glade, Florida, loaded and getting ready to head for New York City; he said Biggy was to load the next day and for me to send the other truck to Roper Growers in Winter Garden to load fruit.

For the next eleven years, or as long as I was in the business, I hauled for Benny Doff, 39 Bronx Terminal Market, New York City. We usually hauled two loads of vegetables from Belle Glade and one load of fruit from Winter Garden a week.

Mr. Doff was good to me and I was good to him. I gave him good service. I have made as many as two or three trips while other trucks were still sitting at a truck broker's. I remember one time the man where I was loading told me he didn't know why Benny was getting the produce that day in Belle Glade because he could buy it cheaper in New York. He said, "Benny said the truck was coming and to load it."

The most alone feeling I have ever had was when I had taken a load of produce from Belle Glade, Florida, to Mr. Doff in New York and he had paid me with a check, as he always did. I had enough cash to get back home, but that was about all I had.

I called Mr. Etheridge, a produce broker in Norfolk, Virginia, who I had hauled for some. He gave me the name of a shipper in Comack, Long Island; I was to go to him and get a load of potatoes and bring them back to Norfolk. It was five o'clock in the afternoon by the time I got the potatoes loaded, got back out on the Long Island Expressway and had that old Mack wound up. I thought to myself, "I can get on back down to Norfolk, get a little sleep in the truck, get unloaded in the morning and have a little time home with my family before I have to go to Florida."

If you have never been on the Long Island Expressway at 5:00 p.m., you can't appreciate the traffic I was in. As I said, I had just gotten the old Mack wound up when I looked out my right rearview mirror and saw a trailer wheel smoking. My heart went in my throat because I knew a wheel bearing was burned out. I didn't have any idea where I could get it fixed, but one thing I did know was I had just enough cash to buy fuel, pay tolls and get a little food to get me home. And cash is the only thing that talks in New York.

The Man Upstairs was with me, as He has been so much of my life. By pulling over a curb, there was room for me to get the truck and trailer off the expressway. Believe me, the only thing those New York cops are worried about is that you are not holding up traffic. I didn't think I was going to ever get a cop to stop, but finally one did. I asked him where I could get some help and he didn't know anything. Remember, there was no such thing as a cell phone then.

The only thing I knew to do was jack the trailer down and go back to the shipper's office and wait until he came down there the next morning. I knew that leaving my trailer was taking a big chance. If they didn't steal it, they would probably steal the potatoes off it, even with the doors locked, but I had no choice. Again, the Man Upstairs was with me. Nothing was stolen. When I got back to the shipper's office, I called Frances on the pay phone and told her my predicament. There was, of course, nothing she could do, but it was so good to hear her voice. It helped me make it through the night, even though there wasn't much sleep. Many times when I was a thousand miles from home, hearing Frances's voice on the phone and knowing she and the kids were okay gave me the strength to keep going. I'm sure this still applies to truckers today; the men and women who haul just about everything we use and yet are some of the lowest paid people for the responsibility they have.

The shipper came down early the next morning. He cashed a freight check for me and called a garage that, I later found out, stayed open all night. The man went to the trailer and repaired it right there and, after paying him $125, I was on my way to Norfolk. I was only getting $100 to take the potatoes to Norfolk, but I was glad to be on my way.

Nowadays, nearly every truck you see is a Peterbilt or Kenworth. I had the first Peterbilt I ever heard of on this part of the coast. They were built on the West Coast and I saw them in Florida, but didn't see them up in the East Coast. The nearest dealer was Hargrave Peterbilt in Orlando. I went to Wachovia bank in Raleigh, where a friend of mine, Dodson Mathias, was working at the time. They said they would finance a White, Mack or International for me, but not a Peterbilt; they had never heard of it. I bought the truck and got it financed with the Associates. It cost $21,000. It had a 318 Detroit diesel.

A few years later, I bought another one and, by this time, they had a dealer in Raleigh. This one cost $25,000. The same tractor today, I am told, would cost well over $100,000. I let Buck Hall, who had been with me about ten years, have this last Peterbilt after I got in the real estate business. Buck wanted to know if I wanted to take a trip with him to Florida. I decided to go, but when we got to Jacksonville on the way south, I told Buck to take me to the airport; I thought I had made my last long-distance trip on a truck. Buck Hall, whom I still consider a good friend, is now retired. Buck was as honest and loyal as anybody who ever worked with me and was the best truck driver I have ever ridden with. He could stay on a truck a week and step out looking just like he had just stepped out of a band box and I would look like I had been through a ringer.

I guess I was fortunate enough to get in the real estate business at the right time in Currituck. The beach was undeveloped and was owned by hunting clubs. You could look as far as you could see in both directions and not see a house. I sold several miles of the beach and a general rule of thumb was "a million dollars a mile."

I carried people to Corolla in a boat and sold oceanfront lots for $12,000 in the fall of 1971. A person I sold one of these lots to turned down $1,000,000 for it in 2005.

For the first house built on the oceanfront in Corolla Village, Ambrose "Hambone" Twiford and I hauled the lumber over there on a barge and carried it out to the oceanfront on a six-wheel army truck that Griggs O'Neal, the deputy sheriff over there, had.

When the road came, the real estate agents came like fleas on a dog's back, and now I'm lost in the fleas.

I have had an interesting and diversified life up to this point and have had the opportunity to do many things I wanted to do. I have had many ups and downs, but all said and done, I have had an enjoyable life. Except for the three years I was in the Coast Guard, I have never had a salary in my life. Every dollar I have had I had to get out and scratch for.

Without the love, devotion and full backing of Frances Meiggs Morris, the things I have managed to enjoy would not have been possible. How she managed to keep a full-time job and raise four children with me gone much of the time is more than I understand to this day.

For those of you who wanted to know, this is how it was to grow up in Currituck, North Carolina.

ALSO AVAILABLE FROM THIS AUTHOR

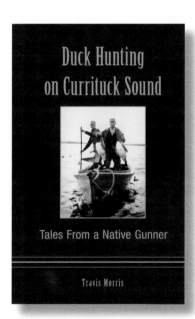

Duck Hunting on Currituck Sound
Tales from a Native Gunner

978-1-59629-167-6 * $19.99 * Sept. 2006

Now in its second printing, this regional bestseller offers an expert's take on the grand history of the area's waterfowl hunting heritage. With stories about Mr. Casey Jones, whose word was "just as good as if it was sworn to you on a stack of Bibles," a 1989 event that became known as the "Piney Island Dove-Hunt-Turned-Turkey-Massacre" in which a neighbor's dog was tried and held accountable on multiple counts of turkey murder and an entry written by Morris's grandson, Chandler Sawyer, about hunting with his grandfather, this collection will delight "gunners" and local history buffs alike.

Please visit us at
www.historypress.net